JOHN BASKERVILLE

A BIBLIOGRAPHY

JOHN BASKERVILLE

A BIBLIOGRAPHY

BY

PHILIP GASKELL

CAMBRIDGE

AT THE UNIVERSITY PRESS

1959

CAMBRIDGE UNIVERSITY PRESS
Cambridge, New York, Melbourne, Madrid, Cape Town, Singapore,
São Paulo, Delhi, Dubai, Tokyo, Mexico City

Cambridge University Press
The Edinburgh Building, Cambridge CB2 8RU, UK

Published in the United States of America by Cambridge University Press, New York

www.cambridge.org
Information on this title: www.cambridge.org/9780521170727

First published 1959
First paperback edition 2010

A catalogue record for this publication is available from the British Library

ISBN 978-0-521-17072-7 Paperback

CONTENTS

Part II: Books

LIST OF ILLUSTRATIONS

IN THE TEXT

BETWEEN PAGES 4 AND 5

BETWEEN PAGES 16 AND 17

* This facsimile is available for download from www.cambridge.org/9780521170727

ABBREVIATIONS

The following abbreviations are used:

Bennett	William Bennett, *John Baskerville, the Birmingham Printer, his Press, Relations and Friends*, 2 vols. (Birmingham, 1937, 1939).
Berry and Johnson, *Catalogue*	W. Turner Berry and A. F. Johnson, *Catalogue of Specimens of Printing Types...1665–1830* (Oxford, 1935).
Berry and Johnson, *Supplement*	W. Turner Berry and A. F. Johnson, 'A Note on the Literature of British Type Specimens with a Supplement to the *Catalogue* [etc.]', *Signature*, New Series 16 (London, 1952), pp. 29–40.
Heawood	Edward Heawood, *Watermarks mainly of the 17th and 18th Centuries* (Hilversum, 1950).
Straus and Dent	Ralph Straus and Robert K. Dent, *John Baskerville, A Memoir* (London, 1907).
Williams, *Letters of Shenstone*	Marjorie Williams, *The Letters of William Shenstone* (Oxford, 1939).

FOREWORD

This book was conceived as a new edition of Straus and Dent's *John Baskerville*, which was to have been edited by Mr R. J. L. Kingsford, Secretary to the Syndics of the Cambridge University Press, and Mr John Dreyfus, Assistant University Printer. Early in 1951 Mr Kingsford decided that the scope of the bibliographical part of the book should be enlarged, and handed that part of the work over to me. I did most of the necessary research during that and the following year. Mr Dreyfus had hoped to have his part of the book—a revision of Straus and Dent's text, together with new material on Baskerville's types—ready for publication in 1958, the bicentenary of Baskerville's appointment as Printer to Cambridge University; but most unfortunately he has been prevented by other duties from completing what was to have been the greater part of the book.

What follows, therefore, is a new Bibliography of specimens and books printed by John Baskerville.

PREDECESSORS

The first published attempt at a bibliography of Baskerville's books is the remarkably good list at the end of H. R. Tedder's article on Baskerville in vol. III of the *Dictionary of National Biography* (London, 1885).[1] Tedder was allowed to use materials collected by the Birmingham antiquary Samuel Timmins, who for many years amassed books and documents from which he hoped one day to write a life of Baskerville. It was a book that was never written, however, and when he died in 1903 he bequeathed his Baskerville materials to Robert Dent. Dent had not got much further when Ralph Straus submitted to him the first draft of a Life and Bibliography of Baskerville. Dent thereupon passed the Timmins materials over to Straus, who wrote the greater part of *John Baskerville, A Memoir*—generally known as 'Straus and Dent'—which appeared in 1907, and which is still the best book on the subject. Straus, who died in 1950, had meant to bring out a new edition of the *Memoir*, and I have had the use of his own interleaved, grangerised and heavily annotated copy. The bulk of the Timmins collection of Baskerville materials is now in the Birmingham Reference Library.

[1] Tedder's list was reprinted, with additions, as the first—and only—pamphlet of the Baskerville Club, a small society of young Cambridge men which included Arthur Cole, Stephen Gaselee, Maynard Keynes and Charles Sayle (*The Baskerville Club: No. 1. Handlist*, Cambridge, 1904).

Attention may also be drawn to the following books and papers about Baskerville's life and work:

J. H. Benton, *John Baskerville, Type-founder and Printer 1706–1775* (Boston, Mass., privately printed, 1914); a new edition, The Typophiles (New York, 1944).

[Beatrice Warde], 'The Roman and Italic of John Baskerville, A Critical Note', *The Monotype Recorder*, vol. XXVI, no. 221 (London, 1927).

William Bennett, *John Baskerville, the Birmingham Printer, his Press, Relations and Friends*, 2 vols. (Birmingham, 1937, 1939).

John Dreyfus, 'The Baskerville Punches 1750–1950', *The Library*, Fifth Series, vol. v (London, 1950), pp. 26–48.

John Dreyfus, 'Baskerville's Ornaments', *Transactions of the Cambridge Bibliographical Society*, vol. I, part ii (Cambridge, 1950), pp. 173–7.

John Dreyfus, 'Baskerville's Methods of Printing', *Signature*, New Series 12 (London, 1951), pp. 44–51.

ACKNOWLEDGMENTS

OF those who have helped me with the preparation of this book I am especially indebted to Lord Rothschild and to the late Mr J. W. Hely-Hutchinson, who allowed me to examine their private Baskerville libraries; to Mr David B. Ellis, Mr James Mosley and Dr M. L. Poston, who lent me rare items from their collections; to Mr R. J. L. Kingsford and to Mr John Dreyfus for their constant encouragement and support; and, most of all, to the following eight people, who, besides helping in many other ways, read the book in proof, and whose labours have resulted in my sending back to the Press a set of galleys containing more additions and corrections than even Baskerville is ever likely to have received: Mr William P. Barlow Jr., of California; Mr David B. Foxon, of the British Museum; Mr Allen T. Hazen, of Yale; Mr Paul Morgan, of Birmingham University Library; Mr A. N. L. Munby, of King's College, Cambridge; Miss Norris, of Birmingham Reference Library; Mr J. C. T. Oates, of Cambridge University Library; and Mr K. Povey, of Liverpool University Library.

PHILIP GASKELL

KING'S COLLEGE, CAMBRIDGE
JANUARY 1958

INTRODUCTION TO THE BIBLIOGRAPHY

THE purposes of this bibliography are first to make it easy to identify all Baskerville's books, pamphlets and broadsides, and secondly to give some information about how they were printed. Thus the full transcriptions of TITLE-PAGES, lists of CONTENTS and the records of ERRORS are included chiefly as aids to identification; while the sections on construction (FORMULA) and on PAPER and TYPE, besides helping with the identification, tell us something about Baskerville's raw materials and about how he used them. I have tried to cut each entry to a minimum while still fulfilling these purposes. A bibliography defeats its end if it is loaded with information which, while it may fascinate the author, is unnecessary to his readers. In certain respects, therefore, my entries are shorter than those that would be appropriate in the bibliography of, say, a seventeenth-century playwright; whereas, since this is the bibliography of a typefounder and printer, not of an author or of a subject, I have said more than usual about type, paper and printing techniques.

Most of the individual sections require a few words of explanation:

TITLE-PAGE, TEXT: Quasi-facsimile transcription is used, as described in chapter 4 of Fredson Bowers, *Principles of Bibliographical Description* (Princeton, New Jersey, 1949).

FORMULA, SHAPE: Bowers's adaptation of Greg's formulary is employed; see chapter 5 of *Principles*.[1] The size of the book is indicated approximately in the eighteenth-century terminology which is still in use today. There are also simplified statements of pagination which do not follow all the Bowers rules but are intended merely as a guide to those who find the formulae difficult. Pages out of series are numbered with arabic figures in square brackets; page numbers within series which must be inferred are *sometimes* italicised, for instance when there is a large number of such pages together or in cases of special difficulty; and when the series is irregular the correct total is given in parentheses at the end.

CONTENTS: More help for those who dislike algebra. These statements generally follow the headlines (or running titles) when there are any, but do not transcribe them literally.

CANCELS: The following terms are used:

Cancellandum (plural *cancellanda*), meaning the leaf that should have been suppressed.

[1] I have made one modification: where a book has more than a few cancels—one issue of the *Ariosto*, for instance, can have sixty-six—they are detailed in a note in parentheses immediately after the plain formula, since the repeated insertion of cancel references in the formula can be cumbersome.

Cancellans (plural *cancellantia*), or 'cancel', meaning the leaf inserted in place of the suppressed leaf.[1]

ERRORS: These entries are not intended to be exhaustive lists of the printers' mistakes; they merely list a few obvious errors, chiefly in the headlines and pagination, which serve to identify particular editions and impressions.

PLATES: Baskerville did not himself engrave or print plates for his books; indeed he used them only rarely in books printed for himself, and he probably had little or nothing to do with the production of the majority of the plates inserted in the books he printed for others. I have therefore not given detailed descriptions of plates, but have merely said where they are usually to be found and have named the engravers and artists concerned when they are known.

PAPER: Sizes in Part I are those of the largest copies seen; nearly all the ephemera appear to have been issued more or less trimmed. In Part II sizes are those of the unfolded and (if there is no qualification) uncut sheet. The following table gives the dimensions in inches of the sizes of paper—more or less standard in the eighteenth century—generally used by Baskerville. The measurements of the uncut, unfolded sheet are given first, followed by the *approximate* dimensions of an uncut book printed on sheets of same size and folded in folio, quarto, octavo and duodecimo. For further information about sizes, watermarks and prices, see Philip Gaskell, 'Notes on Eighteenth-Century British Paper', *The Library*, 5th series, vol. xii (Oxford, 1957), pp. 34–42. The shilling strokes in the descriptions of watermarks divide the descriptions of the main marks from those of the countermarks. Sometimes reference is made to the illustrations of watermarks in Edward Heawood, *Watermarks* (Hilversum, 1950).

	1°		2°		4°		8°		12°	
Super Royal	$27\frac{1}{2}$	$19\frac{1}{4}$	$19\frac{1}{4}$	$13\frac{3}{4}$	$13\frac{3}{4}$	$9\frac{5}{8}$	$9\frac{5}{8}$	$6\frac{7}{8}$	$9\frac{1}{6}$	$4\frac{13}{16}$
Large Printing Royal	26	20	20	13	13	10	10	$6\frac{1}{2}$	$8\frac{2}{3}$	5
Printing Royal	$24\frac{1}{2}$	$19\frac{1}{2}$	$19\frac{1}{2}$	$12\frac{1}{4}$	$12\frac{1}{4}$	$9\frac{3}{4}$	$9\frac{3}{4}$	$6\frac{1}{8}$	$8\frac{1}{6}$	$4\frac{7}{8}$
Writing Royal	24	$19\frac{1}{4}$	$19\frac{1}{4}$	12	12	$9\frac{5}{8}$	$9\frac{5}{8}$	6	8	$4\frac{13}{16}$
Printing Medium	23	18	18	$11\frac{1}{2}$	$11\frac{1}{2}$	9	9	$5\frac{3}{4}$	$7\frac{2}{3}$	$4\frac{1}{2}$
Writing Medium	$22\frac{1}{2}$	$17\frac{1}{2}$	$17\frac{1}{2}$	$11\frac{1}{4}$	$11\frac{1}{4}$	$8\frac{3}{4}$	$8\frac{3}{4}$	$5\frac{5}{8}$	$7\frac{1}{2}$	$4\frac{3}{8}$
Large Printing Demy	$21\frac{1}{4}$	$19\frac{1}{4}$	$19\frac{1}{4}$	$10\frac{5}{8}$	$10\frac{5}{8}$	$9\frac{5}{8}$	$9\frac{5}{8}$	$5\frac{5}{16}$	$7\frac{1}{2}$	$4\frac{13}{16}$
Printing Demy	22	$17\frac{1}{2}$	$17\frac{1}{2}$	11	11	$8\frac{3}{4}$	$8\frac{3}{4}$	$5\frac{1}{2}$	$7\frac{1}{3}$	$4\frac{3}{8}$
Writing Demy	20	$15\frac{1}{2}$	$15\frac{1}{2}$	10	10	$7\frac{3}{4}$	$7\frac{3}{4}$	5	$6\frac{2}{3}$	$3\frac{7}{8}$
Crown	20	15	15	10	10	$7\frac{1}{2}$	$7\frac{1}{2}$	5	$6\frac{2}{3}$	$3\frac{3}{4}$
Post	$19\frac{1}{2}$	$15\frac{1}{4}$	$15\frac{1}{4}$	$9\frac{3}{4}$	$9\frac{3}{4}$	$7\frac{5}{8}$	$7\frac{5}{8}$	$4\frac{7}{8}$	$6\frac{1}{2}$	$3\frac{13}{16}$

TYPE: In Part I (*Specimens, Proposals and other Ephemera*) *all* the type used is noted; in Part II (*Books*), only founts that are used in some quantity, or are of

[1] Dr R. W. Chapman's terminology (*Cancels* (London, 1930), p. 6).

unusual interest.[1] Unless otherwise stated, founts of type and ornaments may be taken to be the ones shown in the *Specimen* of 1775 (no. xvi),[2] of which a facsimile will be found in the pocket inside the lower cover of this book. For the sake of simplicity I have given most of the ornaments descriptive names, which correspond to the numbers given in Straus and Dent (plate XIV) as follows:

'lozenge and star' = Ornament 1	'flower' = Ornament 7
'arabesque' = Ornament 3	'diamond' = Ornament 11
'large rosette' = Ornament 4	'small rosette' = Ornament 14
'fleur-de-lys' = Ornament 6	

LOCATION: The ephemera listed in Part I are nearly all very rare, and I have therefore located all copies known to me of each item. The books in Part II, on the other hand, are for the most part very common; it seems necessary to say no more, therefore, than that all the items listed are to be found in the British Museum, with the following exceptions: nos. 2, 9, 10, 18, 36, 40, 42 and 54, copies of which (with the exceptions of no. 18, which is in the Cambridge University Library, and of no. 40, of which no copy appears to have survived) may be found in the Birmingham Reference Library. In making the Bibliography I have looked at as many copies of each book as I could find; thus I have personally examined over forty copies of no. 1.

NOTES: Included here is such evidence as I have been able to gather of the circumstances of printing and publication, which is not generally very much. I have been through *Aris's Birmingham Gazette* for Baskerville's advertisements, but not through the London papers. I have also gone through *The Gentleman's Magazine* and *The Monthly Review* for notices of Baskerville-printed books.

It will be convenient to add here a priced list of remainders of Baskerville's classics which were offered by Mrs Baskerville in December 1775, when she was trying to sell the whole printing office to a French purchaser:

Terence [46]	860	4to at 10/6	Terence [47]	1000	12mo at 2/3
Catullus [44]	780		Catullus [45]	800	
Lucretius [43]	800		Lucretius [50]	980	
Sallust & Florus [51]	850		Sallust & Florus [55]	800	
Juvenal [15]	250	4to at 6/6	Virgil [34]	800	8vo small at 2/6

N.B. The Quarto lately reduced from 12/6 to 10/6 and the Duodecimo from 2/6 to 2/3. Virgil from 3/- to 2/6.[3]

[1] Only the early uses of the much-employed 'lozenge and star' ornaments are noted.

[2] I have called the fount which is used as a two-line letter with the *Pica* of the specimen *extra caps* (*a*); *extra caps* (*b*) begins the *Long Primer*, and *extra caps* (*c*) the *Bourgeois*.

[3] Bennett, vol. II, p. 55.

The sale did not take place then, however, and the price (£2311. 5*s.*) was reduced to £1100 when the same remainders, or what was left of them, together probably with a remainder of the Shaftesbury [49], were sold to the Worcester bookseller William Smart some time between 1779 and 1784. Smart sold some of the same books to the London bookseller James Robson, who advertised in the *Birmingham Gazette* for 8 November 1784 offering the four quartos of Terence, Catullus, Lucretius and Sallust at 36*s.* the set sewed, stating that the original price of each had been a guinea; and the three octavo volumes of *Characteristicks* at 10*s.* 6*d.*, which had also been published originally at a guinea.[1]

[1] Bennett, vol. II, p. 64.

CONCLUSIONS DRAWN FROM THE BIBLIOGRAPHY

BASKERVILLE spared neither pains nor money to make his books as fine as he could, but his standards of textual accuracy were too low for the results to be entirely successful; most of his books were unusually beautiful, expensive and incorrect.

EQUIPMENT, METHODS OF PRINTING. Baskerville's printing office, even at the end of his life, appears to have been of no more than medium size. He then owned 'Four accurate improved printing presses, several large founts of type, different sizes, with cases, frames, screwed chases, and every other useful apparatus in the branch of trade'.[1] The 'improved presses' were probably of more or less standard English design, but with Blaeu or modified Blaeu hose instead of the normal English box hose.[2] The 'screwed chases' were probably similar to those shown in Simonneau's late-seventeenth-century plates of the special equipment at the Imprimerie Royale.[3] Apart from these relatively minor variations, there is no reason to suppose that Baskerville's printing equipment was in any way abnormal.

Baskerville's book formats were generally in accordance with the usual practice of the time, and ranged in size from Super Royal broadside (no. 56) down to Writing Royal 18° (no. 31); but the problem of the extraordinary make-up of the Post 12° *Horace* of 1762 (no. 23) remains unsolved. He hardly ever used half-sheet imposition, except in duodecimo, which suggests that he was seldom short of type. Analysis of the recurrence of particular headlines (which is easy to make in Baskerville's books owing to the literal errors with which they abound) shows that he did not as a rule use normal skeleton formes (see, for instance, ERRORS in nos. 43, 47 and 55). Baskerville's press-work was not on the whole noticeably better than that of his contemporaries.

TYPE. Baskerville cut and cast his type about a size larger than normal; his *Pica*, for example, was in both face and body about the same size as Caslon's or Wilson's *English*. This is particularly obvious when he used type from another

1 Note of equipment offered by Mrs Baskerville for sale in France in December 1775; Bennett, vol. II pp. 56–7.

2 Letter from Baskerville to Pierres, 2 December 1773; Straus and Dent, pp. 103–4. These presses were not among the equipment that went to Beaumarchais's printing house at Kehl; similar presses were built for Beaumarchais at Saarbrücken, probably with a French modified-Blaeu press as a model; Bib. Hist. de la Ville de Paris, MS. 29602, i, ff. 41–3, 171–2; Bib. Nat., MS. Acq. Nouv. Franç. 6149, ff. 1–2.

3 Reproduced by John Dreyfus in *Signature*, new ser. 12 (London, 1951), p. 51.

foundry together with his own; for instance, in no. 49 he used what looks like Caslon's *Long Primer* Greek in footnotes set in his own *Bourgeois* roman. All his text types from *English* to *Nonpareil* were abnormal in this way, as the following twenty-line measurements show: *English* (Baskerville) 107 mm./(normal) 93 mm.; *Pica*, 95/83; *Small Pica*, 83½/72; *Long Primer*, 74½/67; *Bourgeois*, 67½/59; *Brevier*, 61/56; *Nonpareil*, 47/42.

The order in which Baskerville cut his first types can be deduced from their appearance in the Virgil Specimens and Proposals, and may be compared with the letters he wrote to Dodsley in 1752–4.[1] In no. i we find only *Canon* roman caps—which Baskerville himself referred to as 'two-lines Great Primer', showing that at that time it was a titling fount without a lower case[2]—*Two-line English* roman caps and the complete fount, in its early state, of *Great Primer* (both cases of roman and italic, and small caps). No. ii adds upper and lower case *Small Pica* roman, *Two-line Double Pica* italic caps and *Double Pica* roman caps. No. iii also has the lower case of *Double Pica* roman, and *Double Pica* italic caps. In the 'Melmoth' Specimen (no. v), published probably in April 1757, Baskerville was able to show *Two-line Double Pica* roman caps, both cases of *English* roman, *Small Pica* italic and *Brevier No. 1* roman. The *Virgil* itself, also published in April 1757, has no fount that was not shown on one of these specimens.

Attention may also be drawn to the swash letters in nos. iii, vi and 11; to the different states of the *Great Primer* (nos. iii and 2); to the first uses of ornaments (probably no. viii; but possibly no. 7 or no. 8) and of Baskerville's *Great Primer* Greek (no. 17); to the use of some of Caslon's exotic founts in nos. 28, 49 and 50; and to the woodcut in no. 38.

Towards the end of his life Baskerville allowed himself to use type that was noticeably worn and broken, especially in the duodecimo classics of 1772–4, notwithstanding his widow's assertion that 'it was Mr. Baskerville's custom to melt the types when they had completed one book, so that he always printed with new letter' (Bennett, vol. II, p. 48).

PAPER. There is no evidence that Baskerville ever owned the cumbrous apparatus of a paper mill; he might have been said to have 'manufactured' his special decorated writing paper, which may account for the few references in contemporary letters to his making paper.[3] He used many different sorts of

[1] Straus and Dent, pp. 94–6.

[2] For an explanation of these terms, see Philip Gaskell, 'Type Sizes in the Eighteenth Century', *Studies in Bibliography*, vol. v (Charlottesville, Virginia, 1953), pp. 147–51.

[3] Baskerville did apparently dabble in the manufacture of silk-paper, although he is not known to have printed on it; see William Bailey (of the Society of Arts), *The Advancement of Arts, Manufactures and Commerce* (London, 1772), pp. 217–18.

paper at his press, some of which is identifiable as deriving from Whatman's mill (nos. 14, 39), and several times mentioned buying printing paper (nos. 12, 35; Straus and Dent, p. 101).

Baskerville used wove paper in only three of his books: nos. 1, 7 and 14. Otherwise he used a wide variety of laid papers, heavy as well as light (preferring the latter for most of his better work), ordinary as well as fine. The sheets of most of his finer books were smoothed after printing by pressing; when printing for others, he offered pressing as an optional extra,[1] but appears seldom to have been asked to do it.

Correction and Cancellation. In a letter written to Dodsley in 1754 Baskerville detailed a scheme of proof-correction which, he said, made it 'scarcely possible for the least difference, even of a point, to escape notice'.[2] Would that he had used it himself, for his books are extraordinary as a group for their textual inaccuracy. When mistakes were discovered in the printed sheets he used cancellation extensively; twenty-four of the fifty-six books have obvious cancels, and some of the others may have had whole sections cancelled. The reasons for cancellation were as slight as to be entirely undetectable (no. 15), and as great as the decision of an author to re-write part of his book in proof (no. 32). Some of the books have only one cancelled leaf; one has the amazing total of sixty-six (no. 48). In spite of all this cancellation numerous errors, large and small, were left uncorrected.

Publication, etc. About half of Baskerville's books (at least twenty-seven out of the fifty-six editions) were printed either for other publishers or 'for the author'. The fact that he was so often employed suggests that Shenstone may have been exaggerating when he wrote to Graves on 2 May 1762: 'The expence of printing a sheet of those commendatory verses at a common press is eighteen shillings and at Baskerville's about three pounds, ten shillings.'[3] Baskerville himself wrote to a friend two years later, with reference to a proposal that he should print Grainger's *Sugar Cane*: 'my price is two Guineas the sheet, without pressing, and two pound seven, to be pressed as other Books which I have printed are. The Difference between 1000 and 500 [copies] is to me inconsiderable as it is only Press Work. I have it not in my power to furnish the Paper.'[4]

Comparison of the retail prices of Baskerville's books with those of other groups of eighteenth-century books shows that he can have charged his customers little more than did the average printer of his day, but that the books he printed for himself were very expensive. The following table compares Baskerville's retail

[1] Straus and Dent, p. 101.

[2] Straus and Dent, pp. 95–6.

[3] Williams, *Letters of Shenstone*, p. 627.

[4] Straus and Dent, p. 101.

prices, in terms of cost per sheet, with the retail prices of the first editions of the poet William Mason (mostly in large formats), 1747–95, and of the small-format reprints of the Foulis press in the period 1742–60.

Pence per sheet				
No. of sheets per edition	Mason's first editions[1]	Foulis's reprints[1]	Baskerville's editions	
			for others	for himself
Under 10	4·6	2	3·7	3·8
10–20	2·7	1·9	3·2	3·8
Over 20	2·6	1·6	2·7	4·2

It shows that Baskerville's outstandingly expensive books were the longer ones printed for himself. Among these, the most costly as a group were the last four quarto classics, the retail prices of which averaged over 6*d.* per sheet.

The sizes of Baskerville's editions are largely a matter for conjecture. We know that he printed 1500 copies of the octavo *Milton* of 1758 for Tonson, together with 700 copies of the quarto (nos. 4 and 5); at least 2000 copies of Dodsley's *Fables* (no. 14); 1250 copies of his own folio *Bible* of 1763 (no. 26); and 4000 of his last octavo *Prayer Book* (no. 20). The list of remainders of December 1775 (p. xvii above) showed stocks of from 780 to 860 copies of the last four quarto classics, and of from 800 to 1000 copies of the last four duodecimo classics; which suggests that the original printings may have been of from 1000 to 1500 copies of the quartos and from 1350 to 2000 of the duodecimos, assuming that Baskerville had managed to sell between a quarter and a half of each edition.

Baskerville does not appear to have issued his own books bound; most of the retail prices we have, indeed, are for books specifically unbound or in sheets.[2] There was a bindery, however, which appears to have been closely associated with Baskerville. A copy of the first edition of the octavo *Prayer Book* (no. 12; with borders, 1760, 6*s.* 6*d.*) belonging to Mr R. J. L. Kingsford is in a fine contemporary binding of mottled blue morocco, gilt, with rather striking end-papers which are marbled to represent blended washes of water colour. What links it with Baskerville is the leather label on the spine which is lettered 'COM MON | *PRAYER*' apparently with sorts of his own *Double Pica* roman and italic

[1] These figures are worked out from prices given in Philip Gaskell, *The First Editions of William Mason* (Cambridge, 1951); Philip Gaskell, 'The Early Work of the Foulis Press and the Wilson Foundry', *The Library*, 5th series, vol. VII (Oxford, 1952), pp. 149–77; and other prices in my notes.

[2] No. 14 was offered at 5*s.* bound, but it was printed for Dodsley, who may well have had it bound in London.

caps. A copy in my possession of the duodecimo *Horace* of 1762 (no. 23) seems to have been through the same bindery as Mr Kingsford's *Prayer Book*: bound in sprinkled calf, gilt, it has endpapers with the same distinctive marbling, and its label appears to have been lettered 'HORATIUS' with Baskerville's *Small Pica* roman caps. The same 'water colour' endpapers have also been found in three books at Birmingham. The first is another morocco-bound octavo *Prayer Book* (1760, Birmingham University Library), but its label is missing. The second is Shenstone's calf-bound copy of Dodsley's *Fables* (1761, also Birmingham University Library), which he procured '*before* the Cuts *were inserted*' (see no. 14, NOTES); it has a label, but this is not lettered in Baskerville type. Finally, Dr B. T. Davis of Birmingham University owns Sarah Baskerville's copy of the 1763 Cambridge *Bible* which had remained until recently in the possession of the Ryland family. It is bound in calf with a leather label that may have been lettered with Baskerville's type—though it is not possible to be certain of this—and it has a large printed book label pasted on to a fly-leaf reading:

SARAH BASKERVILLE, [*extra caps* (*b*)] | *BIRMINGHAM.* [*Double Pica italic*] | 1764. [*Double Pica*][1]

[1] Strictly speaking this book label is another piece of Baskerville's ephemeral printing, but it scarcely merits a separate entry in Part I of the Bibliography.

CONCORDANCE WITH STRAUS AND DENT

The following table shows the correspondence between the entries in the present bibliography and those in the bibliography of Straus and Dent.

Gaskell	Straus and Dent	Gaskell	Straus and Dent
i	—	20	53, 54
ii	1, 4	21	55
iii	2	22	56
iv	2	23	57, 58, 59
iv*a*	2	24	61
v	12	25	62
vi	—	26	65, 66
vii	13, 14	27	67
viii	26, 27	28	68, 69
ix	63	29	60, 70
x	64	30	71, 72, 73
xi	64	31	74
xii	—	32	75
xiii	—	33	76
xiv	—	34	77, 78
xv	96, 97	35	79, 80
xvi	111	36	83
		37	82
1	5, 6, 7, 8, 9, 10	38	84
2	11	39	86, 87
3	20	40	—
4	15, 18	41	85
5	17, 19	42	89
6	21, 22	43	90
7	23, 24	44	91
8	25	45	92
9	28	46	93
10	29	47	94
11	38, 39, 43	48	98, 99, 100, 101
12	30, 31, 32, 33, 34, 35	49	102, 103
13	36, 37, 40, 41, 42	50	104
14	44	51	105
15	45	52	106
16	46	53	107
17	47, 48	54	108
18	49	55	109
19	51, 52	56	110

Straus and Dent nos. 3, 50, 81, 88 and 95 were not found.

PART I

SPECIMENS, PROPOSALS AND OTHER EPHEMERA

PART I: SPECIMENS, PROPOSALS AND OTHER EPHEMERA

i SPECIMEN OF THE 4° *VIRGIL*, 1754

SHAPE: Half sheet of 'Royal 4°': A².

TEXT: [A1ᵛ] PUBLII VIRGILII | MARONIS | BUCOLICA | GEORGICA | ET | AENEIS | *Ad optimorum Exemplarium ſidem* | *recenſita.* | BIRMING HAMIAE, | *Johannes Baſkerville Fuſor Typicus excudebat.* | MDCCLIV.

[A2ʳ] *P. VIRGILII MARONIS* | BUCOLICA | *ECLOGA* I. cui nomen *TITYRUS.* | ARGUMENTUM. | *Quum Virgilius*...[7 lines, *Great Primer* italic solid]...*pulſus. &c.* | MELIBOEUS, TITYRUS. | T [2-line] Ityre tu patulæ... [16 lines, *Great Primer* roman leaded]...læva fuiſſet, | A2 Sæpe

Note: The 'Argument' was omitted and the text of the Eclogue corrected in the quarto of 1757. The first word of the last line has been used here as the catchword; the next line actually begins with 'De'.

TYPE: Caps: *Canon* roman, *Two-line English* roman. Caps and lower case: *Great Primer* roman and italic. Small caps: *Great Primer.*

Note: Great Primer italic caps *J, N, O, Q, R* and *T* are in an early state, and were altered later. Several other punches of the founts shown were also touched up or recut, though less obviously.

PAPER: A good, but very light, flimsy laid, vertical chain lines, no marks, size 18¾ × 12¾ in. (probably a sheet of demy or crown trimmed to *Royal* half-sheet shape).

LOCATION: Only one copy known, the property of Dr M. L. Poston of Exmouth. Dr Poston says that it 'was found in a large folio from the library of Lord Bagot at Blithfield, Staffordshire'. The subscribers' list of the 1757 *Virgil* has the entry 'Will. Bagot Eſq. Blythfield, Staffordſhire'.

NOTES: This is presumably the specimen of a quarto *Virgil* mentioned by Baskerville in his Type Specimen and Proposals for *Virgil* of the same year (no. ii below), where he says: 'All perſons who are inclined to encourage the undertaking, are deſired to send their names to JOHN BASKERVILLE in Birmingham; who will give ſpecimens of the work to all who are deſirous of ſeeing them.'

Nos. i and ii were probably issued by the beginning of 1754 (letter from Baskerville to Dodsley of 16 January 1754, quoted in T. B. Reed, *A History of the Old English Letter Foundries* (ed. A. F. Johnson, London, 1952), pp. 269–70); *The Norwich Mercury* for 7–14 December 1754 has an advertisement by Baskerville for the *Virgil*, in which he offers to deliver specimens.

Plates II–III.

ii TYPE SPECIMEN AND PROPOSALS FOR THE 4° *VIRGIL*, 1754

SHAPE: Single leaf of 'Medium 4°'.

TEXT: A | SPECIMEN | By *JOHN BASKERVILLE* of BIRMINGHAM, | In the County of Warwick, *Letter-Founder and Printer.* | To CNEIUS PLANCIUS. | I [2-line] Am indebted to you...[10 lines, *Great Primer* roman leaded]...freely to ſupport | To *CAIUS CASSIUS*, proquæſtor. | *M* [2-line] *Y own inclinations*... [9 lines, *Great Primer* italic solid]... | *ces you requeſt.* | TO THE PUBLIC. | J [2-line] OHN BASKERVILLE propoſes,...[12 lines, *Small Pica* roman solid]...MDCCLIV.

Note: The text of the specimen is taken from William Melmoth's translation of Cicero's *Letters to his Friends* (3 vols., London, 1753).

Type: Caps: *Canon* roman, *Two-line Double Pica* italic, *Two-line English* roman, *Double Pica* roman. Caps and lower case: *Great Primer* roman and italic, *Small Pica* roman. Small caps: *Great Primer.*

Paper: Medium quality laid, vertical chain lines, no marks, size 11½ × 8¼ in. (probably trimmed).

One of the two copies in the Birmingham Reference Library is printed on a piece of coarse brown packing or frisket paper, which is so small (9¼ × 5¾ in.) that the first two lines are cut off.

Location: Birmingham Reference Library (2), St Bride Foundation (2).

Notes: Reproduced (minus the first line) in *The Monotype Recorder*, vol. xxvi, no. 221 (London, Sept.–Oct. 1927), p. 9; and T. B. Reed, *A History of the Old English Letter Foundries* (ed. A. F. Johnson, London, 1952), p. 270.

iii SPECIMEN OF THE 4° *VIRGIL*, WITH PROPOSALS, 1754

Shape: Half sheet of [?] Writing Royal 4°: π^2.

Text: [π 1v] PUBLII VIRGILII | MARONIS | BUCOLICA | GEORGICA | ET | AENEIS | *Ad optimorum Exemplarium fidem recenſita.* | TO THE PUBLIC. | *J* [2-line] *OHN BASKERVILLE propoſes*,...[13 lines, *Great Primer* italic solid] ... | *them.* | Subſcriptions are alſo taken in, and ſpecimens delivered by Meſſieurs R. and | J. DODSLEY, Bookſellers in Pall Mall, London. MDCCLIV.

[π 2r] *P. VIRGILII MARONIS* | BUCOLICA | *ECLOGA* I. cui nomen *TITYRUS.* | Meliboeus, Tityrus. | T [2-line] Ityre, tu patulæ...[24 lines, *Great Primer* roman leaded]...magna ſolebam.

Type: Caps: *Canon* roman, *Two-line Double Pica* italic '*J*', *Two-line English* roman, *Double Pica* italic. Caps and lower case: *Double Pica* roman, *Great Primer* roman and italic, *Small Pica* roman. Small caps: *Great Primer.*

Note: A number of the sorts, particularly in the *Great Primer* italic, have already been altered from the early form found in the plain specimen of *Virgil* of 1754 (no. i above); *Great Primer* italic *N*, *O*, *R* and *T*, for instance, are considerably changed.

The *Double Pica* swash *E* of '*ECLOGA*' on π 2 is very similar to the swash *F* on the last page of the first edition of the 1757 *Virgil.*

The *Two-line Double Pica* italic swash *J* on π 1v is a primitive form with a sloping cross-bar.

Paper: A stoutish laid, horizontal chain lines, no marks, foxed, size 17¼ × 11 in.; referred to in the Proposals as '*this writing royal paper*'.

Location: St Bride Foundation.

Notes: The text of the Proposals is almost, but not quite, the same as that of the Type Specimen and Proposals for *Virgil*, 1754 (no. ii above).

P. VIRGILII MARONIS

BUCOLICA

ECLOGA I. cui nomen *TITYRUS.*

MELIBOEUS, TITYRUS.

Tityre, tu patulæ recubans ſub tegmine fagi,
Silveſtrem tenui Muſam meditaris avena:
Nos patriæ fines, et dulcia linquimus arva,
Nos patriam fugimus: tu Tityre lentus in umbra
Formoſam reſonare doces Amaryllida ſilvas.
T. O Melibœe, Deus nobis hæc otia fecit:
Namque erit ille mihi ſemper Deus; illius aram
Sæpe tener noſtris ab ovilibus imbuet agnus:
Ille meas errare boves, ut cernis, et ipſum
Ludere quæ vellem, calamo permiſit agreſti.
M. Non equidem invideo; miror magis: undique totis
Uſque adeo turbatur agris. en ipſe capellas
Protenus æger ago: hanc etiam vix Tityre duco.
Hic inter denſas corylos modo namque gemellos,
Spem gregis, ah! ſilice in nuda connixa reliquit.
Sæpe malum hoc nobis, ſi mens non læva fuiſſet,
De cœlo tactas memini prædicere quercus.
Sæpe ſiniſtra cava prædixit ab ilice cornix.
Sed tamen, iſte Deus qui ſit, da, Tityre, nobis.
T. Urbem, quam dicunt Romam, Melibœe; putavi
Stultus ego huic noſtræ ſimilem, quo ſæpe ſolemus
Paſtores ovium teneros depellere fœtus.
Sic canibus catulos ſimiles, ſic matribus hædos
Noram; ſic parvis componere magna ſolebam.

PLATE I. Specimen of the 4° *Virgil*, with Proposals, 1754: the third setting. $\pi 2^{r}$. No. iv*a*.
(Cambridge University Library: reduced to 0·74 of original size.)

PUBLII VIRGILII
MARONIS

BUCOLICA
GEORGICA

E T

AENEIS

Ad optimorum Exemplarium fidem recensita.

BIRMINGHAMIAE,

Johannes Baskerville Fusor Typicus excudebat.

MDCCLIV.

PLATES II and III. First Specimen of the 4° *Virgil*, 1754. A1ᵛ and A2ʳ. No. i.
(Dr M. L. Poston: reduced to 0·73 of original size.)

P. VIRGILII MARONIS

BUCOLICA

ECLOGA I. cui nomen *TITYRUS.*

ARGUMENTUM.

Quum Virgilius, cujus perſonam hic ſuſtinet Tityrus paſtor, agrum vicinum Cremonae amiſiſſet, Romam venit: ubi quum ſua eum carmina Maecenati commendaſſent, Mæcenas autem Auguſto, agrum recuperavit. Tityrum igitur felicem eſſe praedicat paſtor Melibœus (ſub cujus nomine ceteri quoque paſtores Mantuani intelliguntur) & ſuam contra calamitatem deplorat, finibus ſuis a milite veterano pulſus. &c.

MELIBOEUS, TITYRUS.

Tityre tu patulæ recubans ſub tegmine fagi,
Silveſtrem tenui Muſam meditaris avena:
Nos patriæ fines, et dulcia linquimus arva,
Nos patriam fugimus: tu Tityre lentus in umbra
Formoſam reſonare doces Amaryllida ſilvas.
T. O Melibœe, Deus nobis hæc otia fecit:
Namque erit ille mihi ſemper Deus; illius aram
Sæpe tener noſtris ab ovilibus imbuet agnus:
Ille meas errare boves, ut cernis, et ipſum
Ludere quæ vellem, calamo permiſit agreſti.
M. Non equidem invideo; miror magis: undique totis
Uſque adeo turbatur agris. en ipſe capellas
Protenus æger ago: hanc etiam vix Tityre duco.
Hic inter denſas corylos modo namque gemellos,
Spem gregis, ah! ſilice in nuda connixa reliquit.
Sæpe malum hoc nobis, ſi mens non læva fuiſſet,

PROPOSALS

For PRINTING by

SUBSCRIPTION.

THE

POETICAL WORKS

OF

JOHN MILTON.

IN TWO VOLUMES.

From the Text of

THOMAS NEWTON D.D.

BIRMINGHAM

Printed by JOHN BASKERVILLE for

J. and *R. TONSON* in *LONDON.*

MDCCLVII.

CONDITIONS.

The book will be printed in two Volumes octavo, on the fame Paper and with the fame letter as the Specimen annexed; the price to Subfcribers (whofe names will be prefixed to the work) will be fifteen Shillings in Sheets; one half to be paid down at the time of fubfcribing, and the remainder on delivery of the Volumes.

N B. The ufual allowance will be given to the trade.

Subfcriptions are taken in by *Meffieurs J.* and *R. Tonfon* in the Strand. *R.* and *J. Dodfley* in Pall Mall London; *Meffieurs Flaćton* in Canterbury, *Mr. Thorn* in Exeter; *Meffieurs Hamilton* and *Balfour* in Edinburgh. *Mr. Fowlis* in Glafcow and by all Bookfellers in Town and Country who by giving a line may have Propofals fent them. And alfo by *John Bafkerville* at his houfe in *Birmingham. To whom Gentlemen who choofe to encourage the undertaking are defired to fend their names.* Where the curious in *Writing Paper* may be *furnifhed* with Superfine poft gilt or plain, *glazed* or *unglazed* of his own manufacture, little inferior in fmoothnefs to the fineft abortive Vellum. He alfo fells quarto poft gilt and beautifully decorated in the borders, at two Shillings and fix-pence the quire, octavo ditto at one Shilling and fix-pence: and Meffages at eight-pence the dozen; and makes large allowance to wholefale dealers.

J. BASKERVILLE returns thanks to the Gentlemen who honored him with their Names to his Edition of Virgil; and begs thofe who have not received their Volume to give a line either to himfelf or Mr. Dodfley in Pall Mall, and they fhall be immediately fupplied.

175 *Received of*

Seven Shillings and fix-pence being the firft payment for Milton's Poetical Works in two Volumes, which I promife to deliver in Sheets on payment of the like Sum.

PLATE IV. First Specimen of *Milton*, with Proposals, 1757. Title-page (*a*) and A 1v. No. vii.

iv SPECIMEN OF THE 4° *VIRGIL*, WITH PROPOSALS, 1754

SHAPE: Half sheet of [?] Printing Demy 4°: π^2.

TEXT: [Exactly as that of no. iii, reset, but with the Proposals themselves in 12 lines instead of 13; i.e. the word '*them.*', which has a line to itself in no. iii, has here been got into line 12. Otherwise the only textual change is the addition of a comma after the word '*hundred*' in line 8 of the Proposals.]

TYPE: As no. iii, but the *E* of '*ECLOGA*' on $\pi 2$ not swash. This change makes the page very similar in appearance to p. 1 of *Virgil*, 1757—of which only the *cancellans* has been seen—the only major changes made there being the removal of line 24 to p. 2, and the indentation of the speech headings.

PAPER: Medium quality laid, horizontal chain lines, watermark a fleur-de-lys, size of sheet at least $20\frac{1}{4} \times 15\frac{1}{2}$ in.

LOCATION: Bodleian Library, Oxford.

iv*a* SPECIMEN OF THE 4° *VIRGIL*, WITH PROPOSALS, 1754

SHAPE: Half sheet of [?] Printing Demy 4°: π^2.

TEXT: [Very closely similar to no. iv; the Proposals in 12 lines, '*hundred*' followed by a comma, and a plain instead of a swash '*E*' on $\pi 2$. It is, however, an entirely new setting. The two can only be told apart by the word 'tactas' in line 17 of the First Eclogue, which in no. iv is set with the ligature 'ct', and in no. iv*a* with separate 'ct'.]

PAPER: Medium quality laid, horizontal chain lines, no marks; fairly heavily cut down, but possibly the same paper as that of no. iv.

LOCATION: Cambridge University Library (Yorke. c. 227[8]).

NOTES: The only known example of this specimen is cut down, folded and inserted in a copy of *The Monthly Review* for December 1754 between sections 2F and 2G. Offset from pp. 448 and 449 (2F8[v] and 2G1[r]) on to the Specimen strongly suggests that this example was inserted into this copy of the magazine at a very early stage, perhaps even before it was issued. There is no reference to the Specimen in the text of the *Review*.

Plate I.

v TYPE SPECIMEN, [1757]

SHAPE: Single leaf of 'Royal 4°'.

TEXT: A | SPECIMEN | By *JOHN BASKERVILLE of Birmingham.* | [the remainder of the text in two columns]
[column 1] I [2-line] Am indebted...[9 lines, *Great Primer* roman solid]...to

the Firft, | I [2-line] Am indebted...[9 lines, *English* roman solid]...Country and to | I [2-line] Am indebted...[9 lines, *Small Pica* roman solid]...as maintaining | *Q. HORATII FLACCI* | Hac ego...[13 lines, *Brevier No. 1* roman solid]...Philippus agendis

[column 2] *if to mean*...[9 lines, *Great Primer* italic solid]...*inforce them;* | approve that...[9 lines, *English* roman solid]...the leaft fha- | *my Authority;*... [9 lines, *Small Pica* italic solid]...*without difficulty,* | *EPISTOLARUM LIBER* I. | Clarus, ab... [13 lines, *Brevier No. 1* roman solid]... negotia, Campo.

TYPE: Caps: *Two-line Double Pica* roman, *Two-line English* roman. Caps and lower case: *Great Primer* roman and italic, *English* roman, *Small Pica* roman and italic, *Brevier No. 1* roman.

PAPER: Good quality thin laid, no marks, vertical chain lines, size at least 11¾ × 8¾ in. (probably trimmed).

LOCATION: Fitzwilliam Museum, Cambridge; Oxford University Press; John Rylands Library, Manchester.

NOTES: Reproduced in W. Turner Berry and A. F. Johnson, *Catalogue of Specimens of Printing Types...1665–1830* (Oxford, 1935), Plate 3 (the O.U.P. copy).

The text in English is again from Melmoth's translation of Cicero's *Letters* (see no. ii above). The date is suggested by a letter written to Baskerville by Robert Dodsley on 7 April 1757, in which he says: 'In the specimen from *Melmoth* I think you have used too many Capitals, which is generally thought to spoil the beauty of printing; but they should never be used to adjectives, verbs, or adverbs' (T. B. Reed, *A History of the Old English Letter Foundries* (ed. A. F. Johnson, London, 1952), p. 272). Dodsley could scarcely have been referring to the earlier Melmoth specimen, which has hardly any capitals; and this one does indeed have far too many, at the beginning of verbs and adjectives as well as of nouns.

vi LORD SHREWSBURY'S CASE, 1757

SHAPE: Half sheet of [?] Writing Royal, folded once: π^2. Imposed for secondary folding as a legal document, with the title across the lower part of $\pi 2^v$; the leaves now separated.

TITLE: *GEORGE BOWES,* Efq. | APPELLANT. | *GEO.* Earl of *SHREWS BURY,* | and others, | RESPONDENTS. | CASE | of the | *RESPONDENT* | *GEO.* Earl of *SHREWSBURY.* | To be heard at the Bar of the | Houfe of Lords on the day | of 175 | BIRMINGHAM, | *Printed by* JOHN BASKERVILLE. | MDCCLVII.

TEXT: [On all four pages; signed on $\pi 2^v$] *E. WILLES.* | *FRA. INGRAM.*

Swash type in no. vi original size

E. WILLES.

FRA. INGRAM.

TYPE: Caps: *Canon* roman initial 'B'; *Two-line Double Pica* roman; *Double Pica* roman and italic, including a swash '*F*' as used on the last page of the first edition of the 1757 *Virgil*. Caps and lower case: *Great Primer* roman and italic, *English* roman and italic.

PAPER: Good quality laid, chain lines vertical to text, horizontal to title, no marks seen; size of sheet at least 23½ × 17½ in. The chain and wire lines are almost obliterated, and the paper bears a marked likeness to that used for the quarto issue of the 1758 *Milton*, although it is probably part of a larger sheet.

Title of no. vi original size

GEORGE BOWES, Efq.

APPELLANT.

GEO. Earl of *SHREWSBURY*,

and others,

RESPONDENTS.

CASE

of the

RESPONDENT

GEO. Earl of *SHREWSBURY*

To be heard at the Bar of the
Houfe of Lords on the day
of 175

BIRMINGHAM,

Printed by JOHN BASKERVILLE.

MDCCLVII.

LOCATION: British Museum.

NOTES: This lawsuit was begun in 1753, when George Bowes claimed part of the estate of a Roman Catholic named Talbot (who had died in 1743) which had gone to Gilbert, the previous Earl of Shrewsbury, as presumed next-of-kin. Bowes disputed this, claiming that he, not the

Earl of Shrewsbury, was the heir-at-law. The case was heard in the Court of Chancery on 22 February 1757, but Bowes's suit was dismissed on account of a technicality connected with the disposal of the estate of a Roman Catholic. He appealed to the Lords, where his case was again dismissed, on 10 February 1758 (Bowes *v.* Shrewsbury (Earl of) 5 Bro. P.C. 144 [E.R. 2. 588]).

vii SPECIMEN OF *MILTON*, WITH PROPOSALS, 1757, 1758

SHAPE: One sheet of [? Writing Royal] 8°: A8.

TITLE-PAGE: [The title-page is found in four states: (*a*) without the words 'VOLUME *the* FIRST', dated 'MDCCLVII'; (*b*) without the words 'VOLUME *the* FIRST', dated 'MDCCLVIII'; (*c*) with the words 'VOLUME *the* FIRST', dated 'MDCCVII'; (*d*) with the words 'VOLUME *the* FIRST', dated 'MDCCLVII'.]

[*a*] PROPOSALS | For PRINTING by | *SUBSCRIPTION.* | THE | POETICAL WORKS | OF | *JOHN MILTON.* | IN TWO VOLUMES. | From the Text of | *THOMAS NEWTON D.D.* | *BIRMINGHAM* | Printed by JOHN BASKERVILLE for | *J.* and *R. TONSON* in *LONDON.* | MDCCLVII.

[*b*] [As (*a*), but with the last line reading 'MDCCLVIII.']

[*c*] [As (*a*) down to line 8, then:] From the TEXT of | *THOMAS NEWTON D.D.* | VOLUME *the* FIRST. | *BIRMINGHAM* | Printed by JOHN BASKERVILLE for | *J.* and *R. TONSON* in *LONDON.* | MDCCVII.

[*d*] [As (*c*), but with the last line reading 'MDCCLVII.']

TEXT: Apart from A1, which has the title on the recto and 'Conditions' on the verso, the whole pamphlet is printed from the type that was used, with minor changes, for A3–A4, b6–b8 and c1–c2 of *Paradise Lost*, 8°, 1758 (no. 4 below).

TYPE: Caps: *Two-line Double Pica* roman and italic (early version of the latter), *Two-line English* roman, *Double Pica* italic. Caps and lower case: roman: *Double Pica, Pica, Brevier No. 1*; roman and italic: *Great Primer, English, Small Pica.* Small caps: *Great Primer.*

PAPER: As *Paradise Lost*, 8°, 1758 (no. 4 below).

LOCATION: (*a*) Lord Rothschild; (*b*) not known (Straus and Dent, no. 14); (*c*) Mr David B. Ellis; (*d*) Birmingham Reference Library; Liverpool University Library; Sir Geoffrey Keynes.

NOTE: The receipt in Sir Geoffrey Keynes's copy of (*d*) is dated 16 December 1757, and in that at Liverpool 11 February 1758.

Plate IV.

viii SPECIMEN OF THE *BIBLE*, WITH PROPOSALS, 1759, 1760

SHAPE: One sheet of Super Royal folio: π^2.

TITLE-PAGE: [within a frame of 'lozenge and star' ornaments, within a frame of thin and thick rule] THE | [xylographic] Holy Bible, | *CONTAINING THE* | OLD TESTAMENT | AND | *THE NEW:* | Tranflated out of the | [xylographic] Original Tongues, | And with | The former Tranſlations diligently | Compared and Reviſed, | *By his MAJESTY'S Special Command.* | APPOINTED TO BE READ IN CHURCHES. | [rule of 'lozenge and star' ornaments] | CAMBRIDGE: | Printed by *JOHN BASKERVILLE*, Printer to the *Univerſity.* | MDCCLIX. *CUM PRIVILEGIO.*

[The cuts, and perhaps some of the type as well, were used again for the title-page of the Bible of 1763 (no. 26 below).]

The Proposals, dated 1759, occupy $\pi 1^v$, and are surrounded by 'lozenge and star' ornaments within a plain rule. On $\pi 2^r$ is Genesis i. 1–28 within a large frame of ornaments and thin and thick rule (as on $\pi 1^r$), and with an inner three-quarter frame of ornaments and plain rule. On $\pi 2^v$ is Genesis i. 29–iii. 3 within a frame of thin and thick rule. The double columns of $\pi 1^v$, $\pi 2^r$ and $\pi 2^v$ are separated by vertical rules of ornaments. (The fourth 'Condition' of the Proposals says '*Some will be printed with an Ornament, like the firſt Page of this Specimen* [$\pi 2^r$], *and ſome with plain Lines, like the ſecond* [$\pi 2^v$]*; the Subſcribers are deſired to mention at the time of ſubſcribing which ſort they chooſe.*')

The text pages of the Bible of 1763, as actually printed, did not bear much resemblance to this specimen; the columns were widened, the notes were set at the feet of the pages instead of at the sides and there were no frames or lines, either of ornaments or of plain rules.

VARIANT: The specimen was re-issued with the date on $\pi 1^r$ changed to 'MDCCLX.', and that on $\pi 1^v$ to '*January* I. MDCCLX.' The only other change was the addition of '*Mr. Dodd* in Ave-Mary Lane:' to the list of booksellers who took in subscriptions ($\pi 1^v$).

TYPE: Caps: *Six-line Pica* italic (not shown in the 1775 specimen); *Canon* italic cap '*A*'; roman and italic *Two-line Double Pica* and *Two-line English.* Caps and lower case: *Canon* roman, *Double Pica* roman and italic, *Great Primer* roman and italic. (The text of the specimen in *Great Primer* roman.) Ornaments: 'lozenge and star'.

PAPER: Medium quality laid, no marks, size of sheet 26 × 20 in.

LOCATION: 1759: Cambridge University Press ($\pi 1$ only). 1760: Enschedé en Zonen, Haarlem, Holland (complete), The Royal Library, Stockholm (complete), Birmingham Reference Library ($\pi 1$ only), Mr R. J. L. Kingsford ($\pi 1$ only).

NOTES: In his letter to the Vice-Chancellor of 31 May 1759, Baskerville promised to produce this specimen 'in about six Weeks' (Straus and Dent, p. 99), following the agreement of December 1758.

Alexander Carlyle, writing his *Autobiography* in 1800, says rather surprisingly that Baskerville was 'on hands' with his folio *Bible* in *May 1758*, and that Garbett (who was accompanying Carlyle on his visit to Birmingham) 'insisted on being allowed to subscribe for Home and Robertson';† but it is hard to see what can have been 'on hands', since the agreement with the University was not made for another seven months, and not even a specimen was produced for over a year after this date.

Plates VI–VII.

† Carlyle, *Autobiography* (ed. J. H. Burton, new ed., London, 1910), p. 386. The names of all four men appear in the subscribers' list of the *Bible.*

ix TYPE SPECIMEN WITHOUT BORDER, [*c.* 1760]

SHAPE: [?] Crown broadside.

TEXT: A SPECIMEN | *BY JOHN BASKERVILLE* | *Of BIRMINGHAM* LETTER-FOUNDER *and* PRINTER. | [between alphabets 'A' to 'V' running down on each side—*Two-line Double Pica* roman on the left and *Two-line English* roman on the right—two columns of specimens, roman on the left, the corresponding sizes of italic on the right; the smallest specimens on each side—*Bourgeois* and *Brevier*—are both roman. The text of each begins]

T [2-line, *Double Pica* to *Small Pica*; 3-line, *Long Primer* to *Brevier*] ANDEM aliquando, Quirites!

[and ends with an alphabet, or part of an alphabet, of caps and a full stop; this final stop is sometimes reversed in *Long Primer* italic.]

TYPE: Caps: *Canon* roman, *Two-line Double Pica* roman, *Two-line English* roman and italic; also cap 'T' in roman and italic *Canon, Two-line Double Pica, Two-line Great Primer, Two-line English,* and in 'extra cap (a)' roman. Caps and lower case: Roman and italic *Double Pica, Great Primer, English, Pica, Small Pica* and *Long Primer*; *Bourgeois* roman, *Brevier* roman.

PAPER: Medium quality laid, horizontal chain, no marks; size 17¼ × 13 in.

LOCATION: Birmingham Reference Library (149154, p. 4); Bibliothèque Nationale; Yale University Library; Enschedé en Zonen, Haarlem, Holland.

NOTES: Reproduced in *The Monotype Recorder*, vol. XXVI, no. 221 (London, Sept.–Oct. 1927), pp. 16–17 (reduced); and D. B. Updike, *Printing Types* (2nd edition, Harvard, 1937), vol. II, fig. 270 (reduced).

Concerning the date of this specimen, see Berry and Johnson, *Supplement*, p. 35.

x TYPE SPECIMEN WITH BORDER, [from *c.* 1762, FIRST EDITION]

INTRODUCTION: This specimen, originally dated [*c.* 1765] by Berry and Johnson (*Catalogue*, p. 30), and later [*c.* 1762] (*Supplement*, p. 35), is found in two separate settings; the second edition, moreover, exists in two states. The type from which the second of these states was printed was used again, with little alteration, to print the second page of the specimen of 1775 (no. xv below). It is likely, therefore, that Baskerville kept this sheet in print over a considerable period of time.

SHAPE: Single leaf of 'Medium folio'.

TEXT: [within a frame of 'lozenge and star' ornaments, with corner pieces] A SPECIMEN | By *JOHN BASKERVILLE* of *BIRMINGHAM.* | [two columns of specimens separated by a vertical rule of 'lozenge and star' ornaments, roman on the left, italic on the right, except for *Bourgeois* which has roman on both sides. The text of the specimens is similar to that of no. ix above, but with two-line initials only.]

TYPE: Caps: *Two-line Great Primer* roman; also cap 'T' in roman and italic *Canon, Two-line Double Pica, 'extra cap (a)', Two-line English*; and roman *'extra cap (b)', 'extra cap (c)'*. Caps and lower case: Roman and italic *Double Pica*, *Great Primer*, *English*, *Pica*, *Small Pica*, *Long Primer*, *Brevier*, *Nonpareil*; *Bourgeois* roman. Ornaments: 'lozenge and star', with corner pieces.

PAPER: A smooth, thin laid paper, horizontal chain lines, size 14¾ × 10½ in. (probably trimmed).

LOCATION: Birmingham Reference Library (149154, p. 3); Cambridge University Press.

NOTE: For the differences between the first and second editions, see no. xi below.

Plate V.

xi TYPE SPECIMEN WITH BORDER, [from *c.* 1762, SECOND EDITION]

SHAPE: Single leaf of 'Medium folio'.

TEXT: [As that of the first edition, reset; *Bourgeois* italic is shown in the right-hand column.]

VARIANT: The specimens of *Brevier* roman and italic and of *Nonpareil* roman and italic, and the frame of ornaments, were reset in a second state. The various versions of this sheet may be identified as follows:

	First edition	Second edition	
		First state	Second state (and specimen of 1775)
Great Primer roman alphabet ends	Q.	P.	P.
Pica roman O in alphabet	[undamaged]	[undamaged]	[damaged]
Bourgeois	[roman only]	[roman and italic]	[roman and italic]
Brevier roman text ends	comparabitur.	comparabitur	atque qui
Brevier italic text ends	*ſine*	*contro-*	*controtroverſa·*
Nonpareil roman text ends	verſabi-	verſa-	verſabit.
Nonpareil italic last line	[full]	[full]	[short]

TYPE: As for the first edition, plus *Bourgeois* italic. The *Pica* roman 'O' is undamaged in the Chicago copy, which probably means that the damage occurred during the original printing of the second state.

PAPER: As for the first edition, size 16¼ × 11¼ in. (Chicago).

LOCATION: First state: Cambridge University Library; Bibliothèque Nationale. Second state: Birmingham Reference Library (154931, p. 79); Newberry Library, Chicago.

xii LATIN LETTER FROM CAMBRIDGE UNIVERSITY, 1762

SHAPE: Royal broadside.

TEXT: *Sereniſſimo Principi,* | *FERDINANDO IV.* | *Utriuſque Siciliae Hieroſolymorumque* | *REGI* | *Hiſpaniarum Infanti;* | *&c. &c. &c.* [followed by 38 lines of text]
[Dated] *DATAE* | *e Senaculo noſtro* | *Pridie* | *Calendas Maias,* | *M DCC LXII* [30 April 1762].
[Signed] *SUMUS,* | *REX SERENISSIME,* | *Omni obſervantiæ pietatiſque ſtudio* | *Celſitudini tuæ devinctiſſimi,* | *Procancellarius,* | *Reliquuſque Senatus,* | *ACADE MIAE CANTABRIGIENSIS.*

TYPE: Caps and lower case: italic *Double Pica, Great Primer* and *Pica*; *Small Pica* italic caps.

PAPER: The Cambridge copy on vellum, decorated with binders' tools and with two painted initials, size 24 × 16½ in. The British Museum copy on laid paper, laid down, size 23¼ × 17¼ in.

LOCATION: Cambridge University Press; British Museum.

NOTES: This letter was first noticed by G. R. (now Sir George) Barnes, who wrote as follows to *The Times Literary Supplement*:

'The document is a Latin letter written by John Skynner, the Public Orator. ... It expresses the thanks of the University to Ferdinand IV., King of the Two Sicilies, for the gift of two volumes of paintings and a gold coin of Augustus found in Herculaneum. Ferdinand IV., Nelson's King of Naples, was a younger son of Charles III. of Spain, and was at this time only eleven years of age.

The manuscript of the letter is to be found in the Registry records (Epist. Acad. II. 743).'†

This appears to be the only piece of jobbing work that Baskerville did for the University; and it seems likely that he made no charge for it. Three vouchers in the University Archives concern the letter: those of Edward Moor, bookbinder, who on 1 May 1762 put a border of gold upon it (6*s.*) and packed it between two large boards (1*s.* 6*d.*); of John Skynner, the Public Orator and author of the letter, who was paid £4. 16*s.* 6*d.* on 7 June for his expenses in taking it to London; and of William Stephens, who received 10*s.* 6*d.* on 10 July for "illuminating & embellishing" it. But there is no trace amongst the vouchers, or in the University Audit Book, of any payment being made for the cost of printing it or for the vellum and paper used.

The copy at Cambridge was hung in the University Library until 1856, when it was transferred to the Registry, and thence to the University Press.

Plate VIII.

xiii JAMES BOSWELL, VERSES IN THE CHARACTER OF A CORSICAN, 1769

SHAPE: Single leaf of [?] Super Royal folio.

TEXT: VERSES | In the CHARACTER of | A CORSICAN | AT | *SHAKE SPEAR*'s JUBILEE, | At STRATFORD upon AVON, Sept. 7, 1769. | By *JAMES BOSWELL*, Efq. | [followed by text, two columns of twenty-four lines each, separated by a vertical rule of 'lozenge and star' ornaments]

† *The Times Literary Supplement*, 32nd year (London, 1933), p. 732.

TYPE: Caps: *Canon* roman, *Two-line Double Pica* roman, *Two-line Great Primer* roman, *Two-line English* italic, *Double Pica* italic. Caps and lower case: *Two-line English* roman, *Double Pica* roman, *Great Primer* roman, *English* roman and italic.

PAPER: (Photograph only seen.) Size 19½ × 13¾ in.

LOCATION: Yale University Library.

NOTES: Boswell made the following entry in his journal for Thursday, 7 September 1769:

'...This was the night of the Ball in Mask, when I was to appear as a Corsican Chief. I had begun some verses for the Jubilee in that character. But could not finish them. I was quite impatient. I went home and forced myself to exertion and at last finished what I intended. ... There was a fellow called Fulke Weale here, who advertised "Printing at an hour's notice,"... To him I went. But Mr. Angelo's fireworks turned his head, and made him idle. He preferred them to all poetical fire. I then went to the Bookseller and Printer of the Place, Mr Kaiting. He had a lad from Baskerville's at Birmingham, of Scots extraction, his name *Shank*. I found him a clever active fellow; and set him to work directly. He brought me a proof to the Masquerade Ball about two in the morning. But could not get my verses thrown off in time for me to give them about in my Corsican dress.' (James Boswell, *The Malahide Papers*, VIII (privately printed, no place, 1930), 99–100.)

In the same volume of *The Malahide Papers* is a facsimile of a printed sheet of these same verses. It is set in what appears to be a very worn fount of Alexander Wilson's *Small Pica* roman No. 1 (as shown in Wilson's 8° *Specimen* of 1772), and begins:

VERSES, | In the Character of a CORSICAN | At SHAKESPEARE's JUBILEE ['1' for 'I'], | At *Stratford-upon-Avon*, Sept. 6 [*sic*], 1769. | By JAMES BOSWELL, Efq; [followed by text in one column]

This facsimile probably represents what Shank did at 'Kaiting's' printing house in Stratford on the night of 7/8 September 1769. It is possible that he then took a copy back to Birmingham with him, where it was printed by Baskerville, his master, perhaps upon instructions from Boswell.

Plomer does not mention Fulke Weale in his *Dictionary* (p. 48, note † below); but says that there was a bookseller called Keating at Stratford-on-Avon between 1749 and 1772 (p. 144).

Plate IX.

xiv PROPOSALS FOR *ORLANDO FURIOSO*, [FIRST EDITION], 1770

NOTE: Not seen. See Proposals for *Orlando Furioso*, Second Edition, 1772 (no. xv below), VARIANTS.

xv PROPOSALS FOR *ORLANDO FURIOSO*, [SECOND EDITION], 1772

SHAPE: Quarter-sheet of [? Writing Royal] 8°: π^2.

TEXT: [π 1^r] *ROLAND FURIEUX,* | POEME HEROIQUE ITALIEN | *DE L'ARIOSTE,* | Nouvelle ÈDITION en 4 Volumes grand 8°. | [followed by text, ending on π 2^r] À BIRMINGHAM; | Chez JEAN BASKERVILLE | M.DCC.LXXII. | [on π 2^v an advertisement for Conti's edition of 'Gerufalemme liberata', and for Baskerville's 4° *Horace* of 1770 with four plates designed by Gravelot]

No. xv
π 1r
original size

ROLAND FURIEUX,

POEME HEROIQUE ITALIEN

DE L' ARIOSTE,

Nouvelle ÉDITION en 4 Volumes grand 8°.

LES plus fameux Libraires de l' Europe ſemblent avoir formé le projet depuis quelque tems d' ajouter encore à la cèlèbrité des meilleurs Auteurs anciens et modernes, en donnant des nouvelles Èditions de leurs Ouvrages, qui ne laiſſaſſent rien à déſirer pour la correction, le papier, et les caractéres.

L' *Arioſte* meritoit à tous égards d'avoir ſa place dans leur collection. Ce Poëte divin, imprimé plus de cent fois, attendoit encore cette diſtinction. Les Frères *Molini* ont entrepris d' en donner une Èdition qui pourra ſatisfaire les dèſirs du Public, et repondre à la reputation de ce grand Homme. Ils ſe ſont ſervi des Prèſſes du fameux *Baſkerville*, dont tout le monde connoit et admire les Chefs d' oeuvres d' Imprimerie. Cette Èdition ne dementira point celles, qui en ſont dèja ſorties. Cet habile Artiſte a achevé d' imprimer les quatre tomes de l' *Arioſte*. Le format, le

TYPE: Caps: *Two-line Great Primer* roman initial 'L', *Double Pica* italic, *Great Primer* roman. Caps and lower case: *English* roman and italic, *Small Pica* roman and italic.

PAPER: Good quality laid, no watermark seen, size of sheet at least 23¼ × 18½ in.

LOCATION: British Museum (bound in the first volume of an 8° *Orlando Furioso*, C. 70. f. 4).

VARIANTS: Straus and Dent (p. 81) mentioned an issue in Royal 4°, citing a copy at the British Museum; they also said that Straus himself owned a copy of the 8° issue. Since there appears to be no copy of the 4° issue at the British Museum, and since Straus and Dent did not cite the Museum copy of the 8° issue, it seems likely that they got the two muddled up. If so, Straus's copy of the 4° issue has since disappeared.

Graham Pollard, in his *Catalogue of Typefounders' Specimens* [etc.] (Birrell & Garnett Ltd., London, 1928), p. 81, described what appears to have been an earlier edition of these *Proposals*, also in 8° but dated 1770. He quoted a passage from this earlier version which said that the first two volumes of the book were already printed and that the other two would come out during the following December; that is, presumably, in December 1770. Copies of both the 8° and the 4° issues of *Orlando* are known with title-pages dated 1771. The 1772 *Proposals* is concerned chiefly with the plates, which were to be completed by the end of 1773; the majority of copies of *Orlando* have title-pages dated 1773. The present location of this copy of the first edition of the *Proposals* is unknown.

xvi TYPE SPECIMEN, 1775, 1777

SHAPE: One sheet of 'Writing Demy folio': π^2.

TEXT: [π 1^v] [within a frame of 'arabesque' ornaments, with corner pieces] Birmingham, 1775. | A SPECIMEN | Of *BASKERVILLE*'s TYPES. | [rule of 'rectangular' ornaments] | [followed by specimens (*Five-line Pica* to *Two-line English*) and ornaments, ending with a rule of 'small rosette' ornaments]
[π 2^r] [within a frame of 'lozenge and star' ornaments, with corner pieces] A SPECIMEN | Of *BASKERVILLE*'s TYPES. | [two columns of specimens separated by a vertical rule of 'lozenge and star' ornaments, roman on the left, italic on the right. Apart from the second line, this page is printed from the same setting of type as had been used for the second issue of the second edition of the Type Specimen with border [from *c.* 1762] (no. xi above).]

TYPE: As Type Specimen with border [from *c.* 1762], second edition, plus: Caps and lower case: roman *Five-line Pica, Canon, Two-line Great Primer*; roman and italic *Two-line Double Pica, Two-line English.* Ornaments: the full range of Baskerville's ornaments—twenty different units.

PAPER: A very thin laid, now rather foxed, horizontal chain lines, no marks, size (Cambridge; probably trimmed) 15 × 20¼ in.

VARIANT: The sheet was re-issued in 1777 (two years after Baskerville's death) with the following changes:

π 1^v: The first line altered to 'Birmingham, 1777.'; exclamation points for commas and full points in the specimens after 'Quirites'.

π 2^r: The *Brevier* of the first issue is renamed '*Brevier* No. 1' and a '*Brevier* No. 2' (roman only) is added. To make room for it one line has been deleted from each of the specimens, roman and italic, of *Small Pica, Long Primer*, and *Bourgeois*; and two lines each from *Brevier* [No. 1] and *Nonpareil* roman and italic.

Location: 1775: Cambridge University Library; Bibliothèque Nationale (π1 only). 1777: Enschedé en Zonen, Haarlem, Holland.

Notes: A full-size reproduction of the second issue was made for John Dreyfus, *The Survival of Baskerville's Punches* (privately printed, Cambridge, 1949); it has been reprinted and inserted in the pocket inside the lower cover of this book. The illustrations in Straus and Dent were made from the Cambridge University Library copy.

A SPECIMEN

By *JOHN BASKERVILLE* of *BIRMINGHAM.*

Double Pica Roman.

TANDEM aliquando, Quirites! L. Catilinam furentem audacia, ſcelus anhelantem, pe-
A B C D E F G H I J K L M N.

Great Primer Roman.

TANDEM aliquando, Quirites! L. Catilinam furentem audacia, ſcelus anhelantem, peſtem patriæ nefarie molientem, vobis atque huic urbi ferrum flam-
A B C D E F G H I J K L M N O P Q.

Engliſh Roman.

TANDEM aliquando, Quirites! L. Catilinam furentem audacia, ſcelus anhelantem, peſtem patriæ nefarie molientem, vobis atque huic urbi ferrum flammamque minitantem, ex
A B C D E F G H I J K L M N O P Q R S.

Pica Roman.

TANDEM aliquando, Quirites! L. Catilinam furentem audacia, ſcelus anhelantem, peſtem patriæ nefarie molientem, vobis atque huic urbi ferrum flammamque minitantem, ex urbe vel ejecimus, vel emiſimus, vel ipſum egredientem verbis proſe-
A B C D E F G H I J K L M N O P Q R S T U.

Small Pica Roman.

TANDEM aliquando, Quirites! L. Catilinam furentem audacia, ſcelus anhelantem, peſtem patriæ nefarie molientem, vobis atque huic urbi ferrum flammamque minitantem, ex urbe vel ejecimus, vel emiſimus, vel ipſum egredientem verbis profecuti ſumus. abiit, exceſſit, evaſit, erupit. nulla jam per-
A B C D E F G H I J K L M N O P Q R S T U V W X.

Long Primer Roman.

TANDEM aliquando, Quirites! L. Catilinam furentem audacia, ſcelus anhelantem, peſtem patriæ nefarie molientem, vobis atque huic urbi ferrum flammamque minitantem, ex urbe vel ejecimus, vel emiſimus, vel ipſum egredientem verbis profecuti ſumus. abiit, exceſſit, evaſit, erupit. nulla jam pernicies a monſtro illo at-
A B C D E F G H I J K L M N O P Q R S T U V W X Y.

Burgeois Roman.

TANDEM aliquando, Quirites! L. Catilinam furentem audacia, ſcelus anhelantem, peſtem patriæ nefarie molientem, vobis atque huic urbi ferrum flammamque minitantem, ex urbe vel ejecimus, vel emiſimus, vel ipſum egredientem verbis profecuti ſumus. abiit, exceſſit, evaſit, erupit. nulla jam pernicies a monſtro illo atque prodigio mœnibus ipſis intra
A B C D E F G H I J K L M N O P Q R S T U V W X Y Z.

Brevier Roman.

TANDEM aliquando, Quirites! L. Catilinam furentem audacia, ſcelus anhelantem, peſtem patriæ nefarie molientem, vobis atque huic urbi ferrum flammamque minitantem, ex urbe vel ejecimus, vel emiſimus, vel ipſum egredientem verbis profecuti ſumus. abiit, exceſſit, evaſit, erupit. nulla jam pernicies a monſtro illo atque prodigio mœnibus ipſis intra mœnia comparabitur.
A B C D E F G H I J K L M N O P Q R S T U V W X Y Z.

Nonpareil Roman.

TANDEM aliquando, Quirites! L. Catilinam furentem audacia, ſcelus anhelantem, peſtem patriæ nefarie molientem, vobis atque huic urbi ferrum flammamque minitantem, ex urbe vel ejecimus, vel emiſimus, vel ipſum egredientem verbis profecuti ſumus. abiit, exceſſit, evaſit, erupit. nulla jam pernicies a monſtro illo atque prodigio mœnibus ipſis intra mœnia comparabitur. atque hunc quidem unum hujus belli domeſtici ducem ſine controverſia vicimus. non jam inter latera noſtra ſica illa verſabi-
A B C D E F G H I J K L M N O P Q R S T U V W X Y Z.

Double Pica Italic.

TANDEM aliquando, Quirites! L. Catilinam furentem audacia, ſcelus anhelantem, peſtem patriae nefarie moli-
A B C D E F G H I J K L M N.

Great Primer Italic.

TANDEM aliquando, Quirites! L. Catilinam furentem audacia, ſcelus anhelantem, peſtem patriæ nefarie molientem, vobis atque huic urbi ferrum flammamque minitan-
A B C D E F G H I J K L M N O P Q R.

Engliſh Italic.

TANDEM aliquando, Quirites! L. Catilinam furentem audacia, ſcelus anhelantem, peſtem patriæ nefarie molientem, vobis atque huic urbi ferrum flammamque minitantem, ex urbe vel ejecimus, vel emi-
A B C D E F G H I J K L M N O P Q R S T.

Pica Italic.

TANDEM aliquando, Quirites! L. Catilinam furentem audacia, ſcelus anhelantem, peſtem patriae nefarie molientem, vobis atque huic urbi ferrum flammamque minitantem, ex urbe vel ejecimus, vel emiſimus, vel ipſum egredientem verbis profecuti ſumus. abiit, exceſſit, evaſit, eru-
A B C D E F G H I J K L M N O P Q R S T U.

Small Pica Italic.

TANDEM aliquando, Quirites! L. Catilinam furentem audacia, ſcelus anhelantem, peſtem patriæ nefarie molientem, vobis atque huic urbi ferrum flammamque minitantem, ex urbe vel ejecimus, vel emiſimus, vel ipſum egredientem verbis profecuti ſumus. abiit, exceſſit, evaſit, erupit. nulla jam pernicies a monſtro illo atque prodigio
A B C D E F G H I J K L M N O P Q R S T U V W X Y.

Long Primer Italic.

TANDEM aliquando, Quirites! L. Catilinam furentem audacia, ſcelus anhelantem, peſtem patriæ nefarie molientem, vobis atque huic urbi ferrum flammamque minitantem, ex urbe vel ejecimus, vel emiſimus, vel ipſum egredientem verbis profecuti ſumus. abiit, exceſſit, evaſit, erupit. nulla jam pernicies a monſtro illo atque prodigio mœnibus ipſis intra mœnia comparabitur. at-
A B C D E F G H I J K L M N O P Q R S T U V W X Y Z.

Burgeois Roman.

TANDEM aliquando, Quirites! L. Catilinam furentem audacia, ſcelus anhelantem, peſtem patriæ nefarie molientem, vobis atque huic urbi ferrum flammamque minitantem, ex urbe vel ejecimus, vel emiſimus, vel ipſum egredientem verbis profecuti ſumus. abiit, exceſſit, evaſit, erupit. nulla jam pernicies a monſtro illo atque prodigio mœnibus ipſis intra
A B C D E F G H I J K L M N O P Q R S T U V W X Y Z.

Brevier Italic.

TANDEM aliquando, Quirites! L. Catilinam furentem audacia, ſcelus anhelantem, peſtem patriæ nefarie molientem, vobis atque huic urbi ferrum flammamque minitantem, ex urbe vel ejecimus, vel emiſimus, vel ipſum egredientem verbis profecuti ſumus. abiit, exceſſit, evaſit, erupit. nulla jam pernicies a monſtro illo atque prodigio mœnibus ipſis intra mœnia comparabitur. atque hunc quidem unum hujus belli domeſtici ducem ſine
A B C D E F G H I J K L M N O P Q R S T U V W X Y Z.

Nonpareil Italic.

TANDEM aliquando, Quirites! L. Catilinam furentem audacia, ſcelus anhelantem, peſtem patriæ nefarie molientem, vobis atque huic urbi ferrum flammamque minitantem, ex urbe vel ejecimus, vel emiſimus, vel ipſum egredientem verbis profecuti ſumus. abiit, exceſſit, evaſit, [illegible]
A B C D E F G H I J K L M N O P Q R S T U V W X Y Z.

PLATE V. First Type Specimen with Border, [*c.* 1762]. First edition. No. x.
(Cambridge University Press: reduced to 0·64 of original size.)

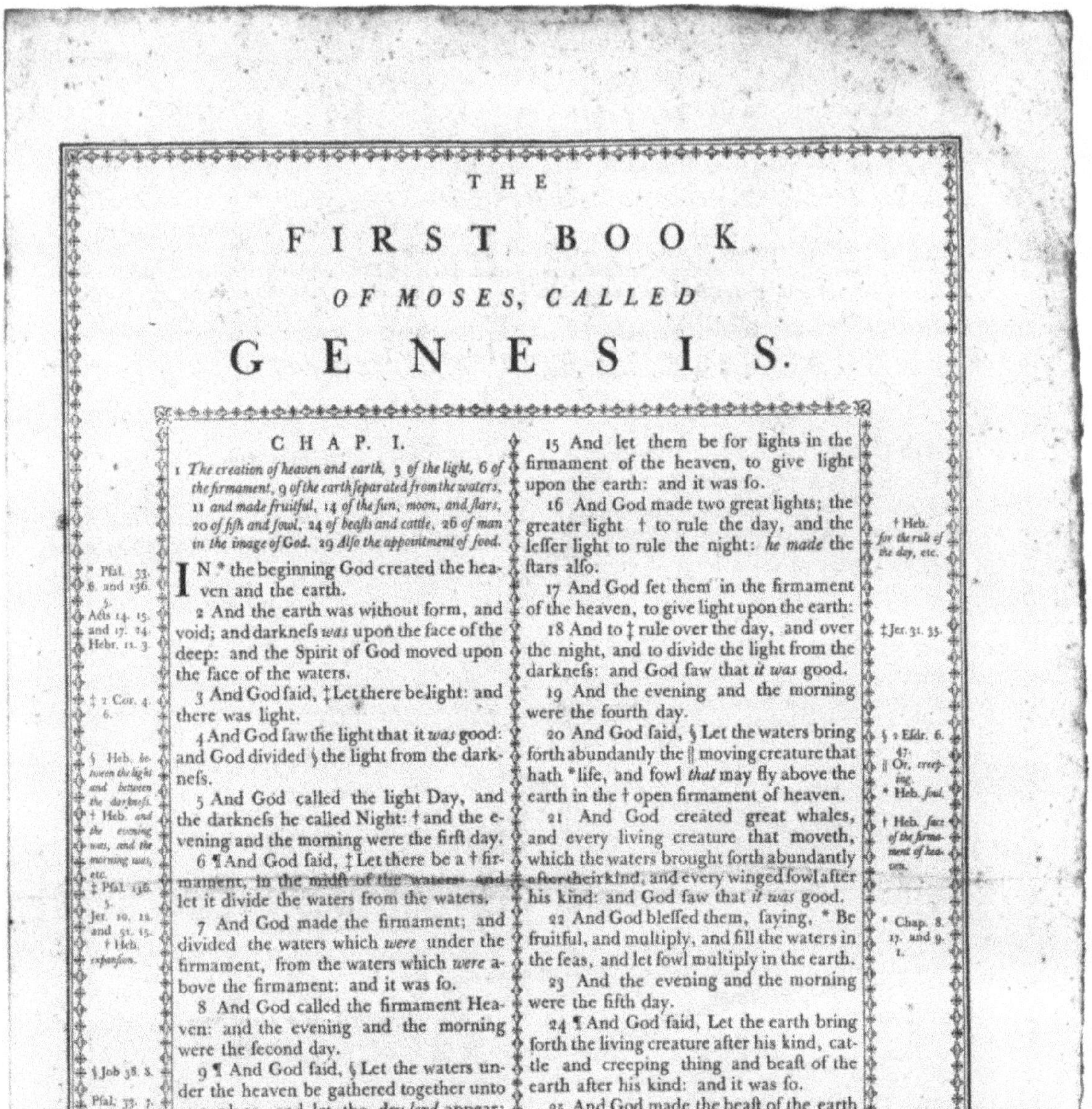

THE

FIRST BOOK

OF MOSES, CALLED

GENESIS.

CHAP. I.

1 The creation of heaven and earth, 3 of the light, 6 of the firmament, 9 of the earth ſeparated from the waters, 11 and made fruitful, 14 of the ſun, moon, and ſtars, 20 of fiſh and fowl, 24 of beaſts and cattle, 26 of man in the image of God. 29 Alſo the appointment of food.

* Pſal. 33. 6. and 136. 5. Acts 14. 15. and 17. 24. Hebr. 11. 3.

IN * the beginning God created the heaven and the earth.
2 And the earth was without form, and
void; and darkneſs *was* upon the face of the
deep: and the Spirit of God moved upon
the face of the waters.

‡ 2 Cor. 4. 6.

3 And God ſaid, ‡ Let there be light: and
there was light.
4 And God ſaw the light that it *was* good:
and God divided § the light from the darkneſs.

§ Heb. *between the light and between the darkneſs.*
† Heb. *and the evening was, and the morning was,* etc.

5 And God called the light Day, and
the darkneſs he called Night: † and the e-
vening and the morning were the firſt day.

‡ Pſal. 136. 5. Jer. 10. 12. and 51. 15.
† Heb. *expanſion.*

6 ¶ And God ſaid, ‡ Let there be a † firmament in the midſt of the waters: and
let it divide the waters from the waters.
7 And God made the firmament; and
divided the waters which *were* under the
firmament, from the waters which *were* a-
bove the firmament: and it was ſo.
8 And God called the firmament Heaven: and the evening and the morning
were the ſecond day.

§ Job 38. 8. Pſal. 33. 7. and 136. 6.

9 ¶ And God ſaid, § Let the waters under the heaven be gathered together unto
one place, and let the dry-*land* appear:
and it was ſo.
10 And God called the dry-*land* Earth;
and the gathering together of the waters
called he Seas: and God ſaw that *it was*
good.

† Heb. *tender graſs.*

11 And God ſaid, Let the earth bring forth
† graſs, the herb yielding ſeed, *and* the fruit-
tree yielding fruit after his kind, whoſe ſeed
is in it *ſelf*, upon the earth: and it was ſo.
12 And the earth brought forth graſs,
and herb yielding ſeed after his kind, and
the tree yielding fruit, whoſe ſeed *was* in
it *ſelf*, after his kind: and God ſaw that *it*
was good.
13 And the evening and the morning
were the third day.

* Deut. 4. 19. Pſal. 136. 7.
† Heb. *between the day and between the night.*

14 ¶ And God ſaid, Let there be * lights
in the firmament of the heaven, to divide †
the day from the night: and let them be
for ſigns, and for ſeaſons, and for days,
and for years.
15 And let them be for lights in the
firmament of the heaven, to give light
upon the earth: and it was ſo.

† Heb. *for the rule of the day,* etc.

16 And God made two great lights; the
greater light † to rule the day, and the
leſſer light to rule the night: *he made* the
ſtars alſo.
17 And God ſet them in the firmament
of the heaven, to give light upon the earth:

‡ Jer. 31. 35.

18 And to ‡ rule over the day, and over
the night, and to divide the light from the
darkneſs: and God ſaw that *it was* good.
19 And the evening and the morning
were the fourth day.

§ 2 Eſdr. 6. 47.
|| Or, *creeping.*
* Heb. *ſoul.*
† Heb. *face of the firmament of heaven.*

20 And God ſaid, § Let the waters bring
forth abundantly the || moving creature that
hath * life, and fowl *that* may fly above the
earth in the † open firmament of heaven.
21 And God created great whales,
and every living creature that moveth,
which the waters brought forth abundantly
after their kind, and every winged fowl after
his kind: and God ſaw that *it was* good.

* Chap. 8. 17. and 9. 1.

22 And God bleſſed them, ſaying, * Be
fruitful, and multiply, and fill the waters in
the ſeas, and let fowl multiply in the earth.
23 And the evening and the morning
were the fifth day.
24 ¶ And God ſaid, Let the earth bring
forth the living creature after his kind, cattle and creeping thing and beaſt of the
earth after his kind: and it was ſo.
25 And God made the beaſt of the earth
after his kind, and cattle after their kind,
and every thing that creepeth upon the
earth after his kind: and God ſaw that *it*
was good.

‡ Chap. 5. 1. and 9. 6. Wiſd. 2. 23. 1 Cor. 11. 7. Epheſ. 4. 24. Col. 3. 10.

26 ¶ And God ſaid, ‡ Let us make man
in our image, after our likeneſs: and let
them have dominion over the fiſh of the
ſea, and over the fowl of the air, and over
the cattle, and over all the earth, and over
every creeping thing that creepeth upon
the earth.

§ Matth. 19. 4.

27 So God created man in his *own* image,
in the image of God created he him: §
male and female created he them.

* Chap. 9. 1.
† Heb. *creepeth.*

28 And God bleſſed them, and God ſaid
unto them, * Be fruitful, and multiply, and
replenish the earth, and ſubdue it: and
have dominion over the fiſh of the ſea, and
over the fowl of the air, and over every
living thing that † moveth upon the earth.

29 ¶ And

Plate VI. Specimen of the Bible, 1760. $\pi 2^r$. No. viii.
(Messrs Enschedé en Zonen, Haarlem: reduced to 0·36 of original size.)

† Heb. *yield-ing ſeed.*
‡ Chap. 9. 3.

29 ¶ And God ſaid, Behold, I have given you every herb † bearing ſeed, which *is* upon the face of all the earth, and every tree, in the which *is* the fruit of a tree yielding ſeed: ‡ to you it ſhall be for meat.

† Heb. *a living ſoul.*

30 And to every beaſt of the earth, and to every fowl of the air, and to every thing that creepeth upon the earth, wherein *there is* † life, *I have given* every green herb for meat: and it was ſo.

§ Ecclus 39. 16.

31 And § God ſaw every thing that he had made, and behold, *it was* very good. And the evening and the morning were the ſixth day.

CHAP. II.

1 *The firſt ſabbath.* 4 *The manner of the creation.* 8 *The planting of the garden of Eden,* 10 *and the river thereof.* 17 *The tree of knowledge only forbidden.* 19, 20 *The naming of the creatures.* 21 *The making of woman, and inſtitution of marriage.*

THUS the heavens and the earth were finiſhed, and all the hoſt of them.

* Exod. 20. 11. and 31. 17. Deut. 5. 14. Hebr. 4. 4.

2 * And on the ſeventh day God ended his work which he had made: and he reſted on the ſeventh day from all his work which he had made.

† Heb. *crea-ted to make.*

3 And God bleſſed the ſeventh day, and ſanctified it: becauſe that in it he had reſted from all his work, which God † created and made.

4 ¶ Theſe *are* the generations of the heavens and of the earth, when they were created; in the day that the LORD God made the earth and the heavens,

5 And every plant of the field, before it was in the earth, and every herb of the field, before it grew: for the LORD God had not cauſed it to rain upon the earth, and *there was* not a man to till the ground.

‖ Or, *a miſt which went up from*, etc.

6 But ‖ there went up a miſt from the earth, and watered the whole face of the ground.

† Heb. *duſt of the ground.*
‡ Ecclus 17. 1. 1 Cor. 15. 47.
§ 1 Cor. 15. 45.

7 And the LORD God formed man † *of* the ‡ duſt of the ground, and breathed into his noſtrils the breath of life; and § man became a living ſoul.

8 ¶ And the LORD God planted a garden eaſt-ward in Eden; and there he put the man whom he had formed.

9 And out of the ground made the LORD God to grow every tree that is pleaſant to the ſight, and good for food: the tree of life alſo in the midſt of the garden, and the tree of knowledge of good and evil.

10 And a river went out of Eden to water the garden; and from thence it was parted, and became into four heads.

* Ecclus 24. 25.

11 The name of the firſt *is* * Piſon: that *is* it which compaſſeth the whole land of Havilah, where *there is* gold.

12 And the gold of that land *is* good: there *is* bdellium and the onyx-ſtone.

† Heb. *Cuſh.*

13 And the name of the ſecond river *is* Gihon: the ſame *is* it that compaſſeth the whole land of † Ethiopia.

‖ Or, *eaſt-ward to Aſſyria.*

14 And the name of the third river *is* Hiddekel: that *is* it which goeth ‖ toward the eaſt of Aſſyria. And the fourth river *is* Euphrates.

‖ Or, *Adam.*

15 And the LORD God took ‖ the man, and put him into the garden of Eden, to dreſs it and to keep it.

† Heb. *eat-ing thou ſhalt eat.*

16 ¶ And the LORD God commanded the man, ſaying, Of every tree of the garden † thou mayeſt freely eat:

† Heb. *dying thou ſhalt die.*

17 But of the tree of the knowledge of good and evil, thou ſhalt not eat of it: for in the day that thou eateſt thereof, † thou ſhalt ſurely die.

† Heb. *as before him.*

18 ¶ And the LORD God ſaid, *It is* not good that the man ſhould be alone: I will make him an help † meet for him.

‖ Or, *the man.*

19 And out of the ground the LORD God formed every beaſt of the field, and every fowl of the air; and brought *them* unto ‖ Adam to ſee what he would call them: and whatſoever Adam called every living creature, that *was* the name thereof.

† Heb. *called.*

20 And Adam † gave names to all cattle, and to the fowl of the air, and to every beaſt of the field: but for Adam there was not found an help meet for him.

21 And the LORD God cauſed a deep ſleep to fall upon Adam, and he ſlept: and he took one of his ribs, and cloſed up the fleſh inſtead thereof.

† Heb. *builded.*

22 And the rib, which the LORD God had taken from man, † made he a woman, and brought her unto the man.

‡ 1 Cor. 11. 8.

23 And Adam ſaid, This *is* now bone of my bones, and fleſh of my fleſh: ſhe ſhall be called Woman, becauſe ſhe was ‡ taken out of man.

§ Matth. 19. 5. Mark 10. 7. 1 Cor. 6. 16. Epheſ. 5. 31.

24 § Therefore ſhall a man leave his father and his mother, and ſhall cleave unto his wife: and they ſhall be one fleſh.

25 And they were both naked, the man and his wife, and were not aſhamed.

CHAP. III.

1 *The ſerpent deceiveth Eve.* 6 *Man's ſhameful fall.* 9 *God arraigneth them.* 14 *The ſerpent is curſed.* 15 *The promiſed ſeed.* 16 *The puniſhment of mankind.* 21 *Their firſt clothing.* 22 *Their caſting out of Paradiſe.*

† Heb. *Yea, becauſe*, etc.

NOW the ſerpent was more ſubtile than any beaſt of the field which the LORD God had made: and he ſaid unto the woman, † Yea, hath God ſaid, Ye ſhall not eat of every tree of the garden?

2 And the woman ſaid unto the ſerpent, We may eat of the fruit of the trees of the garden:

3 But of the fruit of the tree which *is* in the midſt of the garden, God hath ſaid,

Ye

PLATE VII. Specimen of the Bible, 1760. $\pi 2^v$. No. viii.

(Messrs Enschedé en Zonen, Haarlem: reduced to 0·36 of original size.)

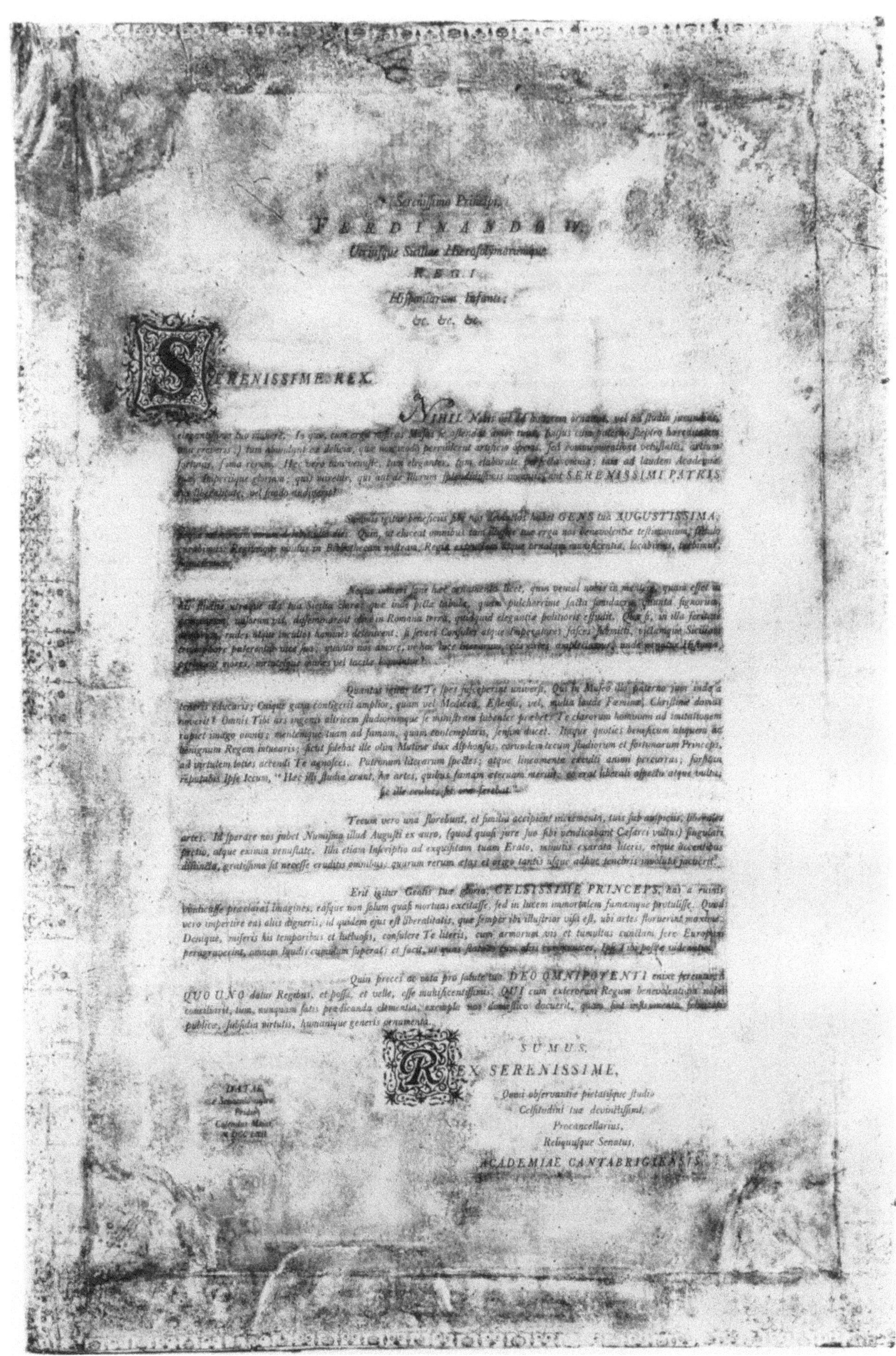

[illegible] Serenissimo Principi,

FERDINANDO IV.

Utriusque Siciliae Hierosolymorumque

REGI

Hispaniarum Infanti:

&c. &c. &c.

SERENISSIME REX.

NIHIL Nobis vel ad [illegible], vel ad studia [illegible] elegantius [illegible]. In quo, cum erga nostras Musas [illegible] ostenderis [illegible] [illegible]) tum abundant [illegible] delicia, [illegible] artificio operas, sed [illegible] vetustatis, artium [illegible], fama rerum. Hæc vero tam vetusta, tam elegantia, tam elaborata [illegible]; [illegible] ad laudem Academiæ [illegible] [illegible] SERENISSIMI PATRIS [illegible] [illegible].

[illegible] GENS tua AUGUSTISSIMA, [illegible] [illegible] erga nos benevolentiæ [illegible] [illegible] in Bibliothecam nostram [illegible] [illegible].

Neque [illegible] [illegible] studiis [illegible] illa tua Sicilia [illegible] tabulæ, quæ pulcherrime facta simulacra, [illegible] signorum, [illegible], [illegible] Romana terra, quidquid elegantiæ politioris effudit. [illegible], in illa [illegible] [illegible], rudes atque incultos homines [illegible]; si severi Consules atque Imperatores fasces submitti, [illegible] Siciliam [illegible] [illegible] [illegible], quanto nos amore, [illegible] [illegible] [illegible] [illegible], [illegible] [illegible] mores, [illegible] [illegible] [illegible]?

Quantas igitur de Te spes susceperint universi, Qui in Museo illo paterno jam inde a teneris educaris; Cuique gaza contigerit amplior, quam vel Medicea, Estensis, vel, multa laude Fœmina, Christinæ domus noverit? Omnis Tibi ars ingenii altricem studiorumque se ministram lubenter præbet: Te clarorum hominum ad imitationem rapiet imago omnis; mentemque tuam ad famam, quam contemplaris, sensim ducet. Itaque quoties beneficum atque [illegible] benignum Regem intuearis; sicut solebat ille olim [illegible] dux Alphonsus, eorundem tecum studiorum et fortunarum Princeps, ad virtutem toties accendi Te agnosces. Patronum literarum spectes; atque lineamenta [illegible] animi percurras; forsitan reputabis Ipse tecum, "Hæc illi studia erant, hæ artes, quibus famam æternam meruit: [illegible] liberali aspectu atque vultu, [illegible] [illegible] [illegible]."

Tecum vero una florebunt, et similia accipient incrementa, tuis sub auspiciis, liberales artes. Id sperare nos jubet Numisma illud Augusti ex auro, (quod quasi jure suo sibi vendicabant Cæsarei vultus) singulari pretio, atque eximia venustate. Illa etiam Inscriptio ad exquisitam tuam Erato, minutis exarata literis, atque decentibus distincta, gratissima sit necesse eruditis omnibus: quarum rerum ætas et origo tantis usque adhuc tenebris involuta jacuerit.

Erit igitur Gentis tuæ gloria, CELSISSIME PRINCEPS, has a ruinis vindicasse præclaras imagines, easque non solum quasi mortuas excitasse, sed in lucem immortalem famamque protulisse. Quod vero impertire eas aliis digneris, id quidem ejus est liberalitatis, quæ semper ibi illustrior visa est, ubi artes floruerint maxime. Denique, miseris his temporibus et luctuosis, consulere Te literis, cum armorum vis et tumultus cunctam fere Europam peragraverint, omnem laudis cumulum superat: et facit, ut quas [illegible] cum aliis [illegible], [illegible] sibi posse videantur.

Quin preces ac vota pro salute tua DEO OMNIPOTENTI enixe [illegible] QUO UNO datur Regibus, et posse, et velle, esse munificentissimis: QUI cum exterorum Regum benevolentiam nobis conciliarit, tum, nunquam satis prædicanda clementia, exemplo nos domestico docuerit, quam sint instrumenta felicitatis publicæ, subsidia virtutis, humanique generis ornamenta.

SUMUS,

REX SERENISSIME,

Omni observantiæ pietatisque studio

Celsitudini tuæ devotissimi,

Procancellarius,

Reliquusque Senatus,

ACADEMIAE CANTABRIGIENSIS.

DATAE

e Senaculo [illegible]

Pridie

Calendas Maii,

[illegible] DCC LXII

PLATE VIII. Latin Letter from Cambridge University, 1762. No. xii.
(Cambridge University Press: reduced to 0·38 of original size.)

VERSES

In the CHARACTER of

A CORSICAN

AT

SHAKESPEAR's JUBILEE,

At STRATFORD upon AVON, Sept. 7, 1769.

By *JAMES BOSWELL*, Esq.

FROM the rude Banks of Golo's rapid Flood,
Alas! too deeply ting'd with Patriot Blood;
O'er which, dejected, injur'd Freedom bends,
And Sighs indignant o'er all Europe sends:
Behold a *CORSICAN!*—in better Days,
Eager I sought my Country's Fame to raise;
When o'er our Camp PAOLI's Banners wav'd,
And all the Threats of hostile France we brav'd,
'Till unassisted, a small Nation fail'd,
And our Invaders tenfold Force prevail'd.
Now when I'm exil'd from my native Land,
I come to join this classic festal Band,
To sooth my Soul on *Avon*'s sacred Stream,
And from your Joy, to catch a chearing Gleam.
To celebrate Great *Shakespear*'s wond'rous Fame
And add new Trophies to the honour'd Name
Of Nature's Bard, whom tho' your Country bore,
His Influence spreads to ev'ry distant Shore:
Wherever genuine feeling Souls are found,
His "Wood Notes wild," with Extasy resound.
Had *Shakespear* liv'd our Story to relate,
And hold his Torch o'er our unhappy Fate;
Liv'd with majestic Energy to tell
How long we fought, what Heroes nobly fell!
Had *Garrick*, who dame Nature's Pencil stole,
Just where Old *Shakespear* dropt it, when his Soul
Broke from its earthy Cage aloft to fly,
To the eternal World of Harmony.
Had *Garrick* shewn us on the Tragic Scene,
With Fame embalm'd our Deeds of Death had been;
If from his Eyes had flash'd the Corsic Fire,
Men less had gaz'd to Pity—than Admire.
O happy *Britons!* on whose favour'd Isle,
Propitious *Freedom* ever deigns to smile,
Whose Fame is wafted on triumphant Gales,
Where thunders War, or Commerce spreads her Sails.
I come not hither sadly to complain,
Or damp your Mirth with melancholy Strain;
In Man's firm Breast conceal'd the Grief should lie,
Which melts with Grace in Woman's gentle Eye;
But let me plead for *Liberty* distrest,
And warm for her each sympathetic Breast:
Amidst the splendid Honours which you bear,
To save a Sister Island! be your Care:
With generous Ardour make *us* also *Free;*
And give to *CORSICA*, *a noble* JUBILEE!

PLATE IX. Boswell's *Verses in the Character of a Corsican*, 1769. No. xiii.
(Yale University Library: reduced to 0·46 of original size.)

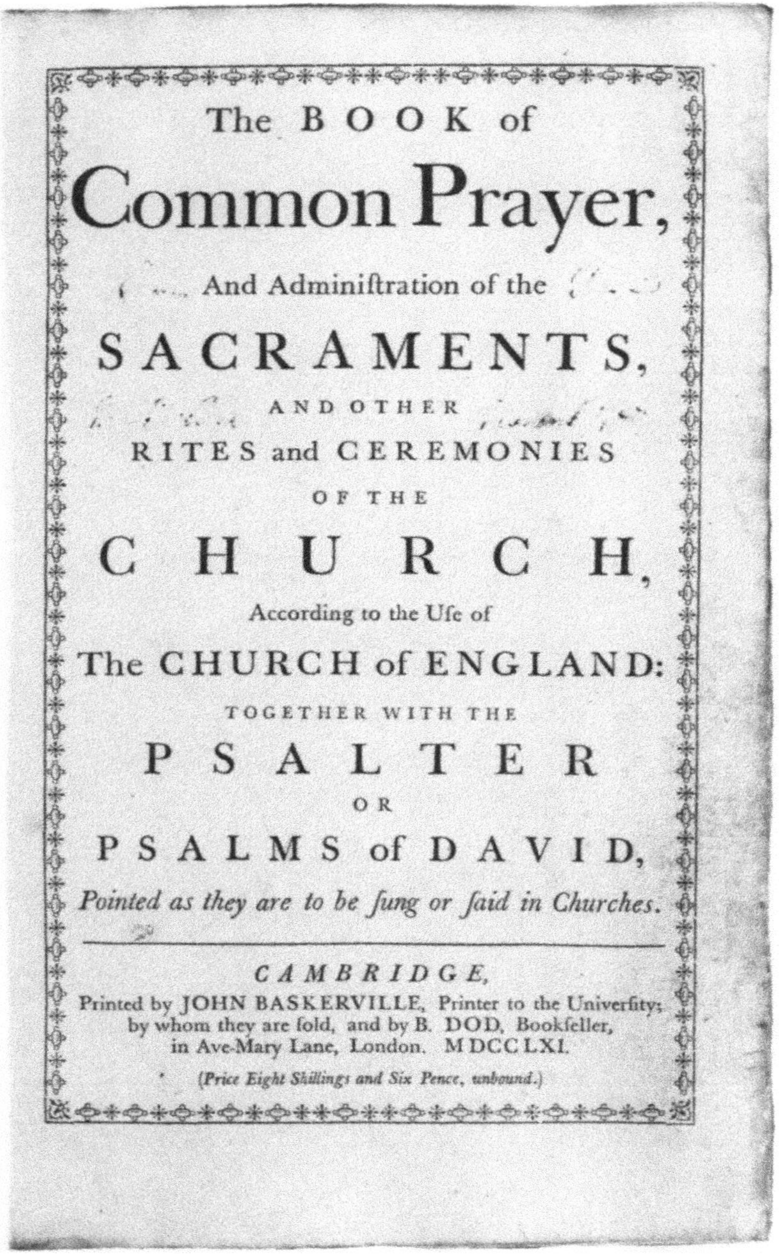

The BOOK of

Common Prayer,

And Adminiftration of the

SACRAMENTS,

AND OTHER

RITES and CEREMONIES

OF THE

CHURCH,

According to the Ufe of

The CHURCH of ENGLAND:

TOGETHER WITH THE

PSALTER

OR

PSALMS of DAVID,

Pointed as they are to be fung or faid in Churches.

CAMBRIDGE,

Printed by JOHN BASKERVILLE, Printer to the Univerfity; by whom they are fold, and by B. DOD, Bookfeller, in Ave-Mary Lane, London. MDCCLXI.

(Price Eight Shillings and Six Pence, unbound.)

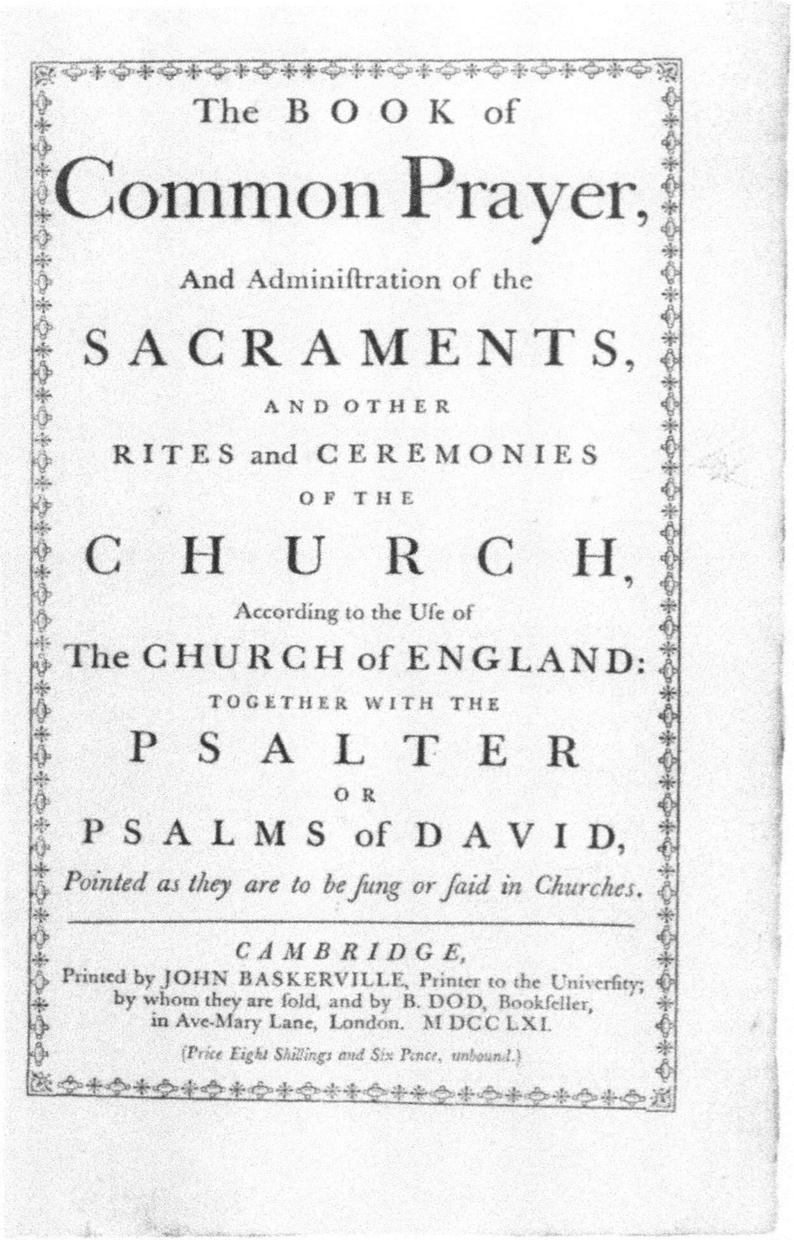

The BOOK of

Common Prayer,

And Adminiftration of the

SACRAMENTS,

AND OTHER

RITES and CEREMONIES

OF THE

CHURCH,

According to the Ufe of

The CHURCH of ENGLAND:

TOGETHER WITH THE

PSALTER

OR

PSALMS of DAVID,

Pointed as they are to be fung or faid in Churches.

CAMBRIDGE,

Printed by JOHN BASKERVILLE, Printer to the Univerfity; by whom they are fold, and by B. DOD, Bookfeller, in Ave-Mary Lane, London. M DCC LXI.

(Price Eight Shillings and Six Pence, unbound.)

PLATE X. The 8° Prayer Books. Two Group 3 title-pages with borders, showing minor variations. Nos. 12 and 13.

(King's College, Cambridge: reduced to 0·71 of original size.)

The BOOK of

Common Prayer,

And Adminiſtration of the

SACRAMENTS,

AND OTHER

RITES and CEREMONIES

OF THE

CHURCH,

According to the Uſe of

The CHURCH of ENGLAND:

TOGETHER WITH THE

PSALTER

OR

PSALMS of DAVID,

Pointed as they are to be ſung or ſaid in Churches.

CAMBRIDGE,

Printed by JOHN BASKERVILLE, Printer to the Univerſity; by whom they are ſold, and by B. DOD, Bookſeller, in Ave-Mary Lane, London. MDCCLXI.

(Price Eight Shillings and Six Pence, unbound.)

The BOOK of

Common Prayer,

And Adminiſtration of the

SACRAMENTS,

AND OTHER

RITES and CEREMONIES

OF THE

CHURCH,

According to the Uſe of

The CHURCH of ENGLAND:

TOGETHER WITH THE

PSALTER

OR

PSALMS of DAVID,

Pointed as they are to be ſung or ſaid in Churches.

CAMBRIDGE,

Printed by JOHN BASKERVILLE, Printer to the Univerſity; by whom they are ſold, and by B. DOD, Bookſeller, in Ave-Mary Lane, London. MDCCLXI.

(Price Eight Shillings and Six Pence, unbound.)

PLATE XI. The 8° Prayer Books. Two Group 3 title-pages without borders, showing minor variations. Nos. 12 and 13.

(King's College, Cambridge: reduced to 0·71 of original size.)

SELECT FABLES
OF
E S O P
AND OTHER FABULISTS.
IN THREE BOOKS.

——*Is not the earth.*
With various living creatures, *and the air*
Replenifhed, and all thefe at thy command
To come and play before thee? Knoweft thou not
Their language and their Ways? They alfo know,
And reafon not contemptibly: with thefe
Find paftime. Paradife Loft. *b.* 8. *l.* 370.

BIRMINGHAM,

Printed by JOHN BASKERVILLE, for
R. and J. DODSLEY in Pall mall. 1761.
Price bound Five Shillings.

PLATE XII. Dodsley's *Select Fables*, 1761. The title opening of

PART II

BOOKS

PART II: BOOKS

I VIRGIL, BUCOLICA, GEORGICA ET AENEIS, 4°, 1757

INTRODUCTION: Baskerville's first and perhaps his finest book is as complicated bibliographically as any that were to follow it from his press. Work on the original edition was in hand by the beginning of 1754, when the first specimens and proposals were issued.† The first twenty-eight sheets (A–2E) were printed on an unwatermarked wove paper, the remainder (2F–3H, π–b) on an unwatermarked laid paper. At some time after the change from wove to laid paper a number of sheets and individual leaves were cancelled, those in the wove sections being easily identifiable through the *cancellantia* being printed on laid paper. Some of these cancels are found in nearly all copies of the book, some in only a few. The book was published in 1757, probably in April, over three years since it had been begun.‡

There was a second edition, textually almost identical with the first, and also dated 1757. Clearly it was intended to be a facsimile of the first edition—it included the original list of subscribers—and, since Baskerville's *Virgil* was soon sought after by eighteenth-century collectors, it is arguable that it was also intended to be sold dishonestly as the first edition. It is difficult to say when it was printed. The later state of the type puts it at least two or three years after the original edition, and it is known that it existed in 1775 when it was mentioned with the implication that it was 'false'.§ Between 1760 and 1775 it is unlikely to have been printed at any press other than Baskerville's, since he is not known to have sold such a wide range of his type to any other printer before his death on 8 January 1775.|| Another indication of the date of the second edition, although an uncertain one, lies in the paper on which it was printed. This is an unwatermarked Writing Royal laid paper, with chain lines 20 mm. apart, that has an unusual and distinctive opacity when held up to the light. The only other occasion on which this particular paper was used at Baskerville's press was in the octavo issue of the Ariosto (4 vols., 1773, but probably printed in 1770; see no. xv above). It was commonly said, early in the nineteenth century, that the second edition was printed in 1771, the earliest mention of this date known to me appearing in the second edition of J-C. Brunet, *Manuel du Libraire*, vol. III (Paris, 1814), p. 423. Renouard adds the following detailed information in 1819: the *Virgil* of 1757, he says, is the most beautiful and the most sought-after of Baskerville's quarto classics, 'malgré la frauduleuse et inférieure réimpression que Baskerville eut la foiblesse de faire sous la même date. Cette édition nouvelle fut tirée au nombre de mille exemplaires¶ pour Elmsly, et pour quelques

† See nos. i–iv *a* above.

‡ Williams, *Letters of Shenstone*, p. 464; Straus and Dent, p. 97.

§ 'The *true* Edition of Baskerville's Virgil sold at Dr *Askew's* sale for 4*l*. 4*s*.' (Edward Harwood, *A View of the Various Editions of the Greek and Roman Classics* (London, 1775), p. 170). The Askew sale took place on 13 February 1775, and the catalogue entry for this item (no. 3324) reads 'Virgilii Opera, *compact. in corio russico, cum foliis deauratis, ac. edit. prima, Birmingh. ap. Baskerville*, 1757' (*Bibliotheca Askeviana* (London, 1775), p. 128).

|| Fry's version of Baskerville's type had been available for some time before 1775, but it differed considerably in detail from the original; the second edition of the *Virgil*, like the first, was printed in Baskerville's own type. Writing to the President of the Royal Academy of Sciences in Paris on 2 December 1773, Baskerville said 'I have never sold any Types, nor do I intend to sell any to London Printers' (Straus and Dent, p. 105).

¶ I am doubtful whether as many as a thousand copies of the second edition were printed, since it appears to be some twenty times less common now than the first edition. There were originally only about five hundred subscribers, so that the first edition is unlikely to have been larger than about two thousand copies, and was probably a good deal smaller.

autres libraires de Londres, qui la payèrent chèrement à l'imprimeur et la vendirent plus chèrement encore, sans avertir que c'étoit une réimpression; jusqu'à ce qu'enfin la fraude découverte mit à leur rang l'édition originale, et son inférieure contrefaçon' (A. A. Renouard, *Catalogue de la Bibliothèque d'un Amateur*, vol. II (Paris, 1819), p. 244).

There are notes on the eleven Yale copies of the 1757 *Virgil* (ten first edition, one second) in Rebecca Dutton Townsend and Margaret Currier, 'A Selection of Baskerville Imprints in the Yale University Library', *Papers in Honor of Andrew Keogh* (New Haven, Conn., privately printed, 1938), pp. 294–6.

Both editions are occasionally found extra-illustrated with a set of plates from Ogilby's translation of *Virgil*, first published in 1654.†

TITLE-PAGE: PUBLII VIRGILII | MARONIS | BUCOLICA, | GEORGICA, | *ET* | AENEIS. | *BIRMINGHAMIAE:* | Typis JOHANNIS BAS KERVILLE. | MDCCLVII.

> *Note:* The title-page is found in two very similar states. In one the 'M' of 'MDCCLVII' is slightly damaged at the top of the left-hand upright; in the other there is slight damage to the top of the 'R' of 'MARONIS' and to the bottom of the 'B' of 'BASKERVILLE'. Tracings suggest that either some of the same type and spacing material was used for both pages, or that one was copied from the other with unusual fidelity. They are found in approximately equal numbers.

FORMULA: Writing Royal 4°: π^2 a–b² A–3H⁴ (with cancels usually at A–B⁴, E4, K4, L1, M3, N1, O1, O3, R1, S3, S4 (*or* T1), Y2, 3B1, 3F4; and, less often, at C⁴, N⁴, 2C⁴, 2F⁴, 2G⁴, 2M⁴ and 3B⁴) [π1—a blank leaf conjugate with the title-page—is frequently missing]. Pp. [12] 1–103 *104–5* 105–231 233–432 [=432].

CONTENTS: π1–π1ᵛ blank, π2 title, π2ᵛ blank, a1–b2ᵛ Subscribers, 1–29 P. Virgilii Eclogae I–X, 30 blank, 31–103 P. Virgilii Georgicon Libri I–IV, 104 blank, 105–432 P. Virgilii Æneidos Libri I–XII.

CANCELS: (*a*) THE USUAL CANCELS.

Cancellanda A–B⁴, E4, K4, L1, M3, O1, O3, R1, S3 and 3B1 not seen.‡

N1: *-andum*, p. 97 l. 380 'Bacchi;', l. 386 'ipſa:'; *-ans*, 'Bacchi,', 'ipſa.'
-andum, p. 98 l. 426 'Ardebat;', l. 420 'reductos;'; *-ans*, 'Ardebat:', 'reductos:'

S4 and T1: in the original setting the last line of S4ᵛ ('Ad ſoceros, et avo puerum Aſtyanacta trahebat.') was repeated as the first line of T1ʳ. In order to correct this, *either* S4 *or* T1 was cancelled, in the first case leaving out the last line of S4ᵛ and in the second leaving out the first line of T1ʳ. *Cancellans* S4 also adds a point at the end of the last line of the recto and gets the numeration of p. 143 right, which was originally printed '341' (and corrected in a few copies of the *cancellandum*); *cancellans* T1 has no other alterations.

Y2: no textual difference between *cancellandum* and *cancellans*, nor any other obvious reason for cancellation.

3F4: *-andum*, p. 416 l. 425 'Iapix'; *-ans*, 'Iapyx'.

† John Ogilby, *The Works of Publius Virgilius Maro translated* (2°, London, 1654 (Wing V610); later 2° editions 1663 (V611) and 1668 (V613)). The plates (which were printed on the same sheets as the letterpress in the seventeenth-century folios) were cut down and mounted for insertion in the Baskerville quartos, thus involving the actual destruction of copies or sheets of Ogilby's book.

‡ Townsend and Currier, *loc. cit.*, also know of an unrevised state of L2–4, which I have not seen.

Note: All the cancels in this section except 3F4 and 3B1 are *cancellanda* when they are on wove paper, *cancellantia* when they are on laid; 3F4 and 3B1 are on laid paper in both states.

(*b*) The uncommon cancels (sheets C, N, 2C, 2F, 2G, 2M and 3B).

C⁴: *-andum*, p. 17 l. 36 'paullatim', l. 37 'ſolem,'; *-ans*, 'paulatim', 'Solem,'
-andum, p. 17 l. 66 'adſurrexerit'; *-ans*, 'aſſurrexerit'
-andum, p. 19 numeration '19', l. 8 'Adſpicio:'; *-ans*, '91', 'Aſpicio:'
-andum, p. 21 subhead '*OCTAVA.*', ll. 6, 14 not indented; *-ans*, '*OCTAVA*', indented
-andum, p. 21 l. 19 'divos'; *-ans*, 'Divos'
-andum, p. 23 l. 59 'aërii', l. 72 'Daphnim'; *-ans*, 'aerii', 'Daphnim.'
-andum, p. 23 l. 75 'deus inpare'; *-ans*, 'Deus impare'
-andum, p. 24 l. 93 'Terra, tibi', l. 99 'alio'; *-ans*, 'Terra tibi', 'olio'
-andum, p. 24 l. 103 'deos,'; *-ans*, 'Deos,'.

N⁴: N1 a new setting, following *cancellans* N1 described above. In N2–4:
-andum, p. 99 headline no point after 'IV'; *-ans*, with point
-andum, p. 101 l. 503 'tranſire' with ligature, 'ſi'; *-ans*, without ligature, 'ſi'
-andum, p. 101 catchword without comma; *-ans*, with comma

2C⁴: *-andum*, p. 200 l. 619 'optata'; *-ans*, 'obtata'
-andum, p. 202 l. 683 'Sidonios,' *-ans*, 'Sidonis,'
-andum, p. 205 l. 44 'Advocat'; *-ans*, 'Avocat'
-andum, p. 206 l. 63 'patrios', p. 207 l. 99 'remiſſos'; *-ans*, 'potrios', 'remiſſes'

2F⁴: *-andum*, p. 227 l. 710 'eſt.'; *-ans*, 'eſt:'

2G⁴: *-andum*, p. 233 l. 866 'aſſiduo longe'; *-ans*, 'aſſido longue'
-andum, p. 235 l. 31 'Partem'; *-ans*, 'partem'

2M⁴: *-andum*, p. 274 l. 328 'monſtrum'; *-ans*, 'Monſtrum'
-andum, p. 277 l. 407 'Latini'; *-ans*, 'latini'
-andum, p. 280 l. 492 normal 'i' in 'quamvis'; *-ans*, dotless w.f. 'i' in 'quamvis'

3B⁴: 3B1 is usually found as a separate *cancellans*, with the reading: p. 378 l. 195, no punctuation at end (original *cancellandum* not seen). When the whole sheet is cancelled, 3B1 is printed from the same setting as the separate *cancellans*, but with a semi-colon at the end of l. 195. The variants in 3B2–4 are as follows:
-andum, p. 379 l. 229 'Latinis'; *-ans*, 'Latinis:'
-andum, p. 381 l. 283 'manus'; *-ans*, 'man us'
-andum, p. 384 l. 388 'undi que'; *-ans*, 'undique'

Note: It will be observed that the majority of the 'uncommon cancel' readings given as corrections are actually less correct than those that they replace. But we can be sure that sheets C, N and 2C are *cancellanda* when they are on wove paper, and *cancellantia* when they are on laid, notwithstanding the fact that most of the changes are *newly-introduced errors*; and, since different settings of sheets 2F, 2G, 2M and 3B are generally found as a group with *cancellantia* sheets C, N and 2C, I have assumed that they too are *cancellantia*, not *cancellanda*. What may have happened was that the original editions of these sheets were underprinted, or partly spoiled, and that the errors were introduced when they were set up for the second time.

Variants: The list of subscribers appears to have been added to during the run. As a rule there is on b2ᵛ a list of four 'Names too late to be inſerted Alphabetically'; but a few copies have lists of either twenty-one or twenty-four additional names.

Errors: Misnumeration: main series runs 1–103 *104–5* 105–231 233–432 (=432). 316 occasionally printed '319'; *cancellandum* S4 usually—but not always—has '341' for 143.

Point missing at end of headline on pp. 93 (*cancellans*), 99, 199, 246 and (sometimes) 225 and 350.

The hyphen after the catchword on p. 233 is nearly always, and on p. 401 always, missing.

The following four errors are rare: b 1r, column 2, 'The Rev. Henry Owen *D.D.*' with the first '*D*' upside down; p. 168, the initial 'F' of the catchword missing; p. 208, the letters 'Dd' of the signature separated by a wide space; and p. 290, headline, 'LIB. VI.' for 'LIB. VII.'

In most copies on p. 134, l. 172, 'arferæ' has been altered by hand to 'arfere', usually by scratching out the final ligature and stamping in the 'e'. The presence of this emendation in an unopened copy (Lord Rothschild) suggests that it was done before the sheets left Baskerville's warehouse.

BIRMINGHAMIAE:

Typis JOHANNIS BASKERVILLE.

MDCCLVII.

First edition, showing damaged 'B' *in* 'BASKERVILLE'

PAPER: Two lots. Sections A–2E on a good quality, rather heavy, unwatermarked *Writing Royal* paper made in a single-faced wove mould,† size of sheet 24½ × 19 in. The remainder of the book, and all *cancellantia*, on a slightly lighter, but otherwise similar, laid paper.

In 1796 James Whatman the younger said that his father, also James Whatman, 'first made the wove paper in 1756' (Thomas Balston in *The Paper Maker*, vol. CXXXI (London, 1956), p. 123). It is not clear whether he meant merely that 1756 was the year in which his father made wove paper for the first time (in which case it might have been invented by someone else), or that it was the year in which his father was the first person to make wove paper. If Whatman made the wove paper for this book, it is likely to have been in 1754 or 1755, rather than in 1756, since the sections on wove paper were printed first. It is possible that the younger James Whatman knew that his father had made the wove paper for the *Virgil*, and that forty years later he had forgotten the exact date of its production, and guessed 1756 because the book was published in 1757.

TYPE: Text, *Great Primer* leaded; Subscribers, *Small Pica*; and see the note on the type of the second edition.

NOTES: Published about April 1757 (p. 19, n. ‡ above); price, one guinea in sheets (advertisement on 2*D*2 of *Horace*, 12°, 1762, no. 23 below). See nos. i–iv *a*, and no. 1 'INTRODUCTION', above.

2 VIRGIL, BUCOLICA, GEORGICA ET AENEIS, [SECOND EDITION], 4°, '1757'

TITLE-PAGE: [Reads as that of the first edition. It can be identified by the position of the 'J' of 'JOHANNIS' in l. 8. In the first edition this is between

† That is, a mould of which the woven wire mesh was fastened directly to the bars, rather than—as was thereafter the case with wove moulds, although not until the end of the century with laid moulds—on top of another wire mesh (double-faced mould). The 'shadows' of the bars are visible in paper made with single-faced moulds; in paper made with double-faced moulds they are not.

the '*B*' and the '*I*' of '*BIRMINGHAMIAE:*' (l. 7); in the second edition it is to the left of the '*B*'.]

FORMULA: [? Printing Royal] 4°: π1 a–b² A–3H⁴ [π1 is here the title-page; no copy seen with a preliminary conjugate blank. Pp. [10] 1–103 *104–5* 105–231 233–432 (=432).

CONTENTS: π1 title, π1ᵛ blank, a1–b2ᵛ Subscribers, 1–29 P. Virgilii Eclogae I–X, 30 blank, 31–103 P. Virgilii Georgicon Libri I–V, 104 blank, 105–432 P. Virgilii Æneidos Libri I–XII.

BIRMINGHAMIAE:

Typis JOHANNIS BASKERVILLE.

MDCCLVII.

Second edition

CANCELS: Although there are no cancels, the following readings may be noted:

From first edition *cancellanda*: sheets 2C, 2F, 2G and 3B (except 3B1).

From first edition *cancellantia*: leaves N1, S4 *and* T1, 3B1 (first version), 3F4; and sheet C.

ERRORS: Misnumeration: main series runs 1–103 *104–5* 105–231 233–432 (=432) as in the first edition; '424' for 224.

Point missing at end of headline on p. 246 as in the first edition. Other first edition errors corrected.

New errors:

Headlines: final point missing on pp. 56, 367; sometimes damaged on pp. 7 and 25; misplaced after the page number on p. 83; inverted on p. 239. 'VIRGLIII' for 'VIRGILII' on pp. 231, 311 and (sometimes) 317.

Catchwords: 'P. VIR.' for 'P. VIR-' on pp. 314, 341, 371 and 401.

Subscribers' list: b1ʳ catchword 'Willam' for 'William'; b2ᵛ, last name in main list, 'Honouable' for 'Honourable'; eighth name in additional list, 'Snrgeon' for 'Surgeon'.

Pp. 143–4: set from the *cancellantia* of both S4 and T1, thereby omitting line 457 entirely.

PAPER: Medium quality laid, no marks; no uncut copy seen, but size of sheet is at least 24 × 18¼ in., so probably *Printing Royal.*

TYPE: As first edition, but in a later state; the set (width of body) of both the *Great Primer* and the *Small Pica* is wider by 6 or 7 per cent; and some of the letters (e.g. the *Double Pica* italic '*Y*' on p. 1, l. 3) are from different punches.

NOTES: See INTRODUCTION to no. 1, above. The second edition, unlike the first, is a rare book. Twenty-four additional subscribers.

3 [JOHN HUCKELL], AVON, 4°, 1758

TITLE-PAGE: AVON | A | POEM | IN | THREE PARTS. | *BIRMINGHAM* | *Printed by* JOHN BASKERVILLE, *and* | *SOLD* | By *R.* and *J. DODSLEY* in *PALL MALL,* | *LONDON.* | MDCCLVIII.

FORMULA: Crown 4°: π^2 A–I⁴ K² [K2 signed]. Pp. [2] 1–78.

CONTENTS: π1–π1v blank, 1 title, 2 blank, 3–78 Avon (p. 28 blank).

ERRORS: All copies seen: p. 30 lacks point in headline; p. 32, note, spells 'Cambden' for Camden; p. 51, l. 408, 'had' omitted after comma. Most copies: K2 signed '2K'. One copy (Yale): p. 13 misnumbered '14'.

PAPER: Medium quality *Crown* laid; watermark, fleur-de-lys/IV; size of sheet 19¾ × 15 in.

TYPE: Text, *Great Primer* leaded.

NOTE: Published about 1 June 1758, price 3*s.* (Straus, *Dodsley*, p. 366; *The Monthly Review*, vol. XIX, p. 272.)

4 JOHN MILTON, PARADISE LOST, 8° AND 4°, 1758

(*a*) OCTAVO ISSUE

TITLE-PAGE: PARADISE LOST. | A | POEM, | IN | TWELVE BOOKS. | The AUTHOR | *JOHN MILTON.* | From the Text of | *THOMAS NEWTON D.D.* | *BIRMINGHAM* | Printed by JOHN BASKERVILLE for | *J.* and *R. TONSON* in *LONDON.* | M DCC LVIII.

FORMULA: [? Writing Royal] 8°: A^8 b^8 c^2 B–$2C^8$ $2D^4$ $2E^2$ (with cancels at G7, H5, P1, T6, T8, X6, Z3 and Z5. Sections a–i (*Life*) from *Paradise Regained*, 1758 (no. 5 below), are sometimes placed between b and c). Pp. [32] 1–416.

CONTENTS: A1–A1v blank, A2 title, A2v blank, A3–A4 Preface, A4v blank, A5–b5v Subscribers, b6 sub-title to Paradise Lost, b6v–b8 poems by Barrow and Marvel, b8v The Verse, 1–416 Paradise Lost Books I–XII (the following pages blank: 32, 102, 142, 178, 214, 312, 390).

CANCELS: A copy in the possession of Mr David B. Ellis has *cancellanda* instead of *cancellantia*, and is also remarkable for having a copy of the Proposals for the book, dated 1757 (no. vii above), bound in instead of sections A, b and c. The following are the main differences:
G7: *-andum*, p. 97 l. 620 'ſharp'nd'; *-ans*, 'ſharpend'
-andum, p. 98 l. 652 'errands over'; *-ans*, 'errands, over'
H5: *-andum*, p. 109 l. 110 'at laſt'; *-ans*, 'at leaſt'
P1: *-andum*, p. 213 l. 900 'Which Satan;', l. 901 'now his'; *-ans*, 'With Satan;', 'now is'
T6: *-andum*, p. 287 headline 'Book XI.'; *-ans*, 'Book IX.'
T8: *-andum*, p. 291 l. 616 'in the'; *-ans*, 'in thee'
X6: *-andum*, p. 320 l. 138 'gav'ſt'; *-ans*, 'giv'ſt'
Z3: *-andum*, p. 345 l. 853 'execution, death as oft accuſed'; *-ans*, 'execution, ſince denounc'd'
Z5: *-andum*, p. 349 l. 946 'peacefull'; *-ans*, 'peaceful'
-andum, p. 350 l. 989 'childleſs'; *-ans*, 'Childleſs'

ERRORS: Some copies: misnumeration '13' for 135; 'dD' for signature Dd [1]; p. 346, headline, roman 'I' in '*PARADISE*'.

Most copies: p. 75, l. 3, 'God his light', usually with the 'h' of 'his' erased by hand. Headlines: p. 160, 'V' for 'V.'; p. 237, 'VII' for 'VII.'; pp. 285, 311, 'XI.' for 'IX.'.

PAPER: Medium quality laid, no marks; size of sheet of a copy of No. 5, octavo issue, is 25 × 19¼ in., so probably *Printing Royal.*

TYPE: Text, *English* leaded; Subscribers, *Small Pica*; Preface, *Great Primer.*

(*b*) QUARTO ISSUE

TITLE-PAGE: [From the same setting as the octavo.]

FORMULA: [? Post] 4°: A^4 b–d^4 e^2 B–$3F^4$ $3G^2$ (with cancels at N3, P1, 2E1, 2O2, 2O4, 2S2, 2X3, 2Y1). Pp. [32] 1–416.

CONTENTS: A1–A1ᵛ blank, A2 title, A2ᵛ blank, A3–A4 Preface, A4ᵛ blank, b1–d1ᵛ Subscribers, d2 sub-title to Paradise Lost, d2ᵛ–d4 poems by Barrow and Marvel, d4ᵛ The Verse, 1–416 Paradise Lost Books i–xii (blank pages as the octavo).

CANCELS: No *cancellanda* seen, but presumably as the octavo.

ERRORS: Some copies: the 'C' of signature 'C3' reversed. All copies: p. 75, l. 3, and headlines pp. 160, 237, 311 as octavo; p. 285 correct; also headline p. 86, 'II' or 'III' for 'III.'.

PAPER: Good quality laid, no marks; no uncut copy seen, but size of sheet is at least $18\frac{3}{4} \times 14\frac{1}{4}$ in., so probably *Post*. It might be mistaken for a wove paper, as the chain and wire marks are almost obliterated, besides being very close together.

NOTE: See Notes to no. 5 below.

5 JOHN MILTON, PARADISE REGAINED, ETC, 8° AND 4°, 1758

(*a*) OCTAVO ISSUE

TITLE-PAGE: PARADISE | REGAIN'D. | A | POEM, | IN | FOUR BOOKS. | To which is added | *SAMSON AGONISTES:* | AND | POEMS upon SEVERAL OCCASIONS. | THE AUTHOR | *JOHN MILTON.* | From the Text of | *THOMAS NEWTON, D.D.* | *BIRMINGHAM:* | Printed by JOHN BASKER VILLE | For *J.* and *R. TONSON* in *LONDON.* | MDCCLVIII.

FORMULA: [? Writing Royal] 8°: π^2 a–i^4(–i4) A–F^8 (F4+χ1) G–$2A^8$ *2B*1 (with cancels at H2, H3, O4, Q8, R8, Y7, Z5, 2A8). Pp. [4] i–lxx 3–100 102–163 *164–6* 166–390 (=390).

CONTENTS: π1–π1ᵛ blank, π2 title, π2ᵛ blank, a1–i3 The Life of Milton, i3ᵛ blank, 3–90 Paradise Regain'd Books i–iv (pp. 4, 24, 26, 46, 64, 66 blank), 91–163 Samson Agonistes (pp. 92, 96 blank), 164–265 Poems on Several Occasions i–xix (p. 212 blank), 266–80 Sonnets i–xxiii, 280–313 Psalms i–cxxxvi (total nineteen), 314 blank, 315–390 Poemata (no headline, p. 316 blank).

CANCELS: *Cancellanda* not seen.

ERRORS: Misnumeration: 'lxiii' for xliii; main series runs 3–100 102–163 *164–6* 166–390 (=390). Headlines: p. 72, '*PARAIDSE*'; 90, '*REAGIN'D*'; 68, 73, '148', '162', lack point.

PAPER: As no. 4, octavo issue.

TYPE: Text, *English* leaded; Life, *Pica*.

(*b*) QUARTO ISSUE

TITLE-PAGE: [From the same setting as the octavo, with some changes in spacing.]

FORMULA: [? Post] 4°: π1 a–i⁴(–i4) A–L⁴(L4+χ1) M–3B⁴ 3C1 (with cancels at 2D4, 2I4, 2L4, 2X3, 2Z1, 3B4). Pp. [2] i–lxx 3–390.

CONTENTS: As the octavo, except:

(*a*) The quarto lacks the initial blank.

(*b*) Samson ends on p. 162, and the Poems on Several Occasions begin on p. 163, because the misnumbering of the octavo has been corrected.

CANCELS: *Cancellanda* not seen. Here P2 and P3 (the H2 and H3 of the octavo) are not cancelled; P was printed from a forme containing the pages that printed the *cancellantia* of the octavo, showing that the original mistakes were discovered before the formes were re-imposed for the quarto printing.

ERRORS: As in the octavo, but with the main series numeration corrected to run 3–390, so that pp. '148' and '162' (where the points are missing from the headlines) are now numbered 147 and 161.

PAPER: As no. 4, quarto issue.

NOTES: William Shenstone to Thomas Percy, letter received 1 December 1758: 'Baskerville's Milton, they tell me comes out in y[e] X[tmas] holidays' (Williams, *Letters of Shenstone*, p. 500). Straus and Dent (pp. 31, 68) give the date of publication of the 8° as 27 January 1758 (this should probably be 1759), the edition size as 1500 copies, and the price as 15*s*. the set; and say that 700 copies of the 4° issue were put out in June at 21*s*. the set (no sources given). In spite of this long delay, the cancels show that, as usual, the two issues were printed concurrently. See no. vii, above.

6 JOHN MILTON, PARADISE LOST, 4°, 1759

TITLE-PAGE: [From the same setting as the title-page of no. 4 (*Paradise Lost*, 1758), with the date changed to 'MDCCLIX'. There is another state with a colon after '*BIRMINGHAM*'.]

Note: Only the title-page is from the setting used for no. 4; the rest of the book is reset.

FORMULA: [? Printing Demy] 4°: π⁴ a–i⁴ A² B–3F⁴ 3G². Pp. [8] i–lxxii 1–416.

CONTENTS: π1 title, π1ᵛ blank, π2 sub-title to Paradise Lost, π2ᵛ–π4 poems by Barrow and Marvel, π4ᵛ The Verse, a1–i4ᵛ The Life of Milton, 1–416 Paradise Lost Books I–XII (blanks as *Paradise Lost*, 1758).

ERRORS: Headlines: p. 36, '*LOSL.*'; 68, 115, '*LSOT.*'; 148, 'V' for 'V.'; 190, '190 Book *PARADISE LOST.* VI.'; 196, 'VI' for 'VI.'; pp. 37, 83, 266, 406 '*LOST*' for '*LOST.*'.

PLATES: There are usually no plates, but occasionally a frontispiece (signed Miller) and set of twelve plates (signed Hayman and Müller) are found, facing π1, A2, E4, K4, O3, T3, 2A1, 2E3, 2H4, 2M1, 2R4, 2Z1, 3D3. They were supplied by Tonson, who distributed several versions of these designs (see C. H. Collins Baker, 'Some Illustrators of Milton's Paradise Lost', *The Library*, 5th series, vol. III (Oxford, 1949), pp. 14–15; Straus and Dent, p. 113).

PAPER: Medium quality laid, no marks; no uncut copy seen, but size of sheet is at least 19¾ × 14½ in., so probably *Printing Demy*.

TYPE: Text, *English* leaded; Life, *Pica*.

7 JOHN MILTON, PARADISE REGAINED, ETC, 4°, 1759

TITLE-PAGE: PARADISE | REGAIN'D. | A | POEM, | IN | FOUR BOOKS. | To which is added | *SAMSON AGONISTES:* | AND | POEMS upon SEVERAL OCCASIONS. | THE AUTHOR | *JOHN MILTON,* | From the TEXT of | *THOMAS NEWTON, D.D.* | *BIRMINGHAM:* | Printed by JOHN BASKER VILLE, for | *J.* and *R. TONSON* in *LONDON.* | M DCC LIX.

Note: In two states, cancelled and uncancelled: in the *cancellandum* the first word in line 8 was printed '*SAMPSON*', then the '*PSON*' was erased and '*SON*' carelessly overprinted, possibly by hand; in the *cancellans* the whole title-page is reset, using some of the same type, '*SAMSON*' correct.

FORMULA: [? Writing Demy] 4°: A^4 (±A^4; A1+χ1 [=3C4]) B–$3C^4$ (–3C4 [=χ1]) [in some copies 3C4 (Table of Contents) is in its original position]. Pp. 1–390 (=392, see 'ERRORS' below).

CONTENTS: A1 title, A1v blank, χ1–χ1v The Table of Contents, A2–90 Paradise Regain'd Books I–IV (pp. 24, 24, 26, 46, 64, 66 blank), 91–162 Samson Agonistes (pp. 92, 96 blank), 163–265 Poems on Several Occasions I–XIX (p. 212 blank), 266–80 Sonnets I–XXIII, 280–313 Psalms I–CXXXVI (total nineteen), 314 blank, 315–90 Poemata (no headline, p. 316 blank).

CANCELS: To correct the faulty title-page of some copies, the whole of section A was cancelled; there is no other textual change.

ERRORS: The numeration runs: [6 (χ1v numbered '4')] 5–254 247 246 248–57 256–7 260–61 260–61 264–390 (=392).
Headlines: pp. 107, 135, lack point; 311, 312, '*PSAL.*' for '*PSALMS.*'; 256 'XVI.' for 'XVII.'; 305 'LXXVII.' for 'LXXVI.'.

PLATES: Occasionally a frontispiece (signed Vertue) and set of five plates (signed Hayman and Grignion) facing A1, A3, N2, 2B2, 2C1, 2E1 (see no. 6, above).

PAPER: Good quality wove, no marks, approximately same size as the paper of no. 6; probably *Writing Demy.*

TYPE: Text, *English* leaded; Contents, *Small Pica.* 'Lozenge and star' ornaments.

8 [JOHN] PIXELL, SONGS, 2°, 1759

TITLE-PAGE: A | *COLLECTION OF* | SONGS, | WITH THEIR | RECITA TIVES | AND | SYMPHONIES, | FOR THE | GERMAN FLUTE, VIOLINS, *etc.* | with a *THOROUGH BASS* for the | HARPSICHORD. | Set to MUSICK by | *Mr. PIXELL.* | To which is added | A *CHORUS* for *VOICES* and *INSTRUMENTS.* | [rule of 'lozenge and star' ornaments] | *BIRMING HAM.* | Printed for the AUTHOR, and fold by *Meff. WALSH* and *JOHNSON.* | LONDON.

COLOPHON: [p. 41] *Engrav'd and Printed by* M. Broome | *in Birmingham* 1759.

FORMULA: [? Short Demy] folio: π1 A^2+21 leaves of engraved music, probably arranged *B–F² G1.* Pp. [6] 1–42.

CONTENTS: (Letterpress:) π1 title, π1ᵛ blank, A1–A2 Subscribers Names, A2ᵛ blank; (engraved:) 1–41 words and music (no headline), 42 blank.

PAPER: Medium quality laid, no marks in the letterpress section; in the engraved section a slightly thicker paper, marks Fleur-de-lys/IV. Size of sheet at least 19½ × 13¼ in., so possibly *Short Demy* (a plate size measuring 20¼ × 14 in.).

TYPE: Title-page, sizes from *Canon* to *Pica*; Subscribers, *Small Pica*. 'Lozenge and star' ornaments.

NOTE: Published probably by 3 October 1759 (Williams, *Letters of Shenstone*, p. 521). Pixell's first name is taken from the second volume of the Registers of Edgbaston church, where he was Vicar from 1750 to 1784. (Publications of the Dugdale Society, vol. XIV (London, 1936), p. x.)

9 JOHN MILTON, PARADISE LOST, 8°, 1760

TITLE-PAGE: PARADISE LOST. | A | POEM, | *IN* | TWELVE BOOKS. | The AUTHOR | *JOHN MILTON.* | From the Text of | *THOMAS NEWTON,* D.D. | [rule of 'star' ornaments] | *BIRMINGHAM:* | Printed by JOHN BASKERVILLE, for | *J.* and *R. TONSON,* in *LONDON.* | MDCCLX.

FORMULA: [? Printing Royal] 8°: a^4 b^4 c^8 A1 B–D^8(±D4) E–$2C^8$ $2D^4$ $2E^2$ [F3 not signed]. Pp. [30] 1–416.

CONTENTS: *a*1–*a*1ᵛ blank, *a*2 title, *a*2ᵛ blank, *a*3–c4 Subscribers, c4ᵛ blank, c5 sub-title to Paradise Lost, c5ᵛ–c7 poems by Barrow and Marvel, c7ᵛ The Verse, 1–416 Paradise Lost Books I–XII (the following pages blank: 32, 102, 142, 178, 214, 312, 390).

CANCEL: D4 *cancellandum* not seen.

ERRORS: Misnumeration: '96' for 69, '131' for 231, '135' for 235, '268' for 262, '230' for 330. Headline: p. 83, 'II.' for 'III.'.

PAPER: Medium quality laid, no marks; no uncut copy seen, but size of sheet is at least 25¼ × 19 in., so probably *Printing Royal.*

TYPE: Text, *English* leaded; Subscribers, *Small Pica.*

NOTE: See Note to no. 10 below.

10 JOHN MILTON, PARADISE REGAINED, ETC, 8°, 1760

TITLE-PAGE: PARADISE | REGAIN'D. | A | POEM, | IN | FOUR BOOKS. | To which is added | *SAMSON AGONISTES*: | AND | POEMS upon SEVERAL OCCASIONS. | THE AUTHOR | *JOHN MILTON.* | From the Text of | *THOMAS NEWTON D.D.* | [rule of 'lozenge and star' ornaments] | *BIR MINGHAM:* | Printed by JOHN BASKERVILLE | For *J.* and *R. TONSON* in *LONDON.* | MDCCLX.

FORMULA: Printing Royal 8°: π^2 2π1 a–i^4 A–F^8(F4+χ1) G–$2A^8$ 2*B*1 (with cancels at i2, H1, P7). Pp. [6] i–lxxii 3–163 *164–6* 166–390 (=389).

CONTENTS: π1–π1v blank, π2 title, π2v blank, 2π1–2π1v The Table of Contents, a1–i4v The Life of Milton, 3–90 Paradise Regained Books I–IV (pp. 4, 24, 26, 46, 64, 66 blank), 91–163 Samson Agonistes, 164–265 Poems on Several Occasions I–XIX (p. 212 blank), 266–80 Sonnets I–XXIII, 280–313 Psalms I–CXXXVI (total nineteen), 314 blank, 315–90 Poemata (p. 316 blank).

CANCELS: i2, H1 and P7. *Cancellanda* not seen.

ERRORS: Main series numeration runs: 3–163 *164–6* 166–390 (=389). Misnumerations, 'lxvii' for xlvii, '161' for 261; sometimes, 'lxviii' for xlviii. Headlines: p. 58, '*PARA EDISE RGAIN'D.*'; p. 77, '*REGAIN D*'; pp. 128, 129, roman 'G' in '*AGONISTES.*'; p. 160, '*N*' of '*AGONISTES.*' broken.

PAPER: As no. 8.

TYPE: Text, *English* leaded; Life, *Pica*.

NOTE: Nos. 9 and 10 were published together on about 5 May 1760, price 21*s*. in sheets (*Birmingham Gazette*, no. 964).

11 [DAVID MALLET], EDWIN AND EMMA, 4°, 1760

TITLE-PAGE: EDWIN, | *AND* | EMMA. | [rule of 'lozenge and star' ornaments] | BIRMINGHAM: | Printed by *JOHN BASKERVILLE*, | for A. MILLAR in the *Strand*. | MDCCLX.

FORMULA: [? Printing Royal] 4°: A–B4. Pp. 1–16.

CONTENTS: 1 title, 2 blank, 3–11 Edwin and Emma, 12 blank, 13–14 Extract of a letter, 15 Advertisement, 16 blank.

PAPER: Medium quality laid; marks, Strasbourg bend over LVG/JW; size of sheet 24¼ × 19 in., so probably *Printing Royal*.

TYPE: Text, *Double Pica* leaded; 'Letter', *Great Primer* and *Pica*. Swash *Two-line English* italic '*A*' on the title-page.

NOTES: Published on about 21 March 1760, price 1*s*. (*The Public Advertiser*); reviewed in *The Monthly Review* for June 1760 (vol. XXII, p. 514).

A remainder of 100 copies of this book, enlarged with a postscript and a set of five plates, was issued in 1810 in dark brown paper boards at £1. 1*s*.† It had an extra title-page reading: *BASKERVILLE'S ORIGINAL EDITION* | OF | EDWIN AND EMMA, | FIRST PRINTED IN THE YEAR | M.DCC.LX. | [thick and thin rule] | THE FEW REMAINING COPIES OF THIS RARE EDITION ARE ILLUSTRATED | BY | LOCAL SUBJECTS, | DRAWN AND ETCHED BY GEORGE ARNALD. | TO WHICH IS ADDED, | THE PARISH REGISTER OF THEIR DEATHS. | [thick and thin rule] | London: | PUBLISHED BY LONGMAN, HURST, REES, ORME, AND BROWN, | PATERNOSTER-ROW. | *Printed by J. M'Creery, Black-Horse-Court, London.* | [plain rule] | 1810.

† Letter from George Arnald in the possession of the late Ralph Straus.

12, 13, 19 THE OCTAVO PRAYER BOOKS, 1760–62

Introduction

Baskerville printed three octavo editions of *The Book of Common Prayer*. The first, which appeared in 1760, was set in long lines of Great Primer.† There were two impressions, one with and the other without a border round each page of his favourite 'lozenge and star' ornament. It was originally published at 6*s*. 6*d*.; cancel title-pages were substituted later in 1760 and in 1761, altering the price to 7*s*. 6*d*. and 8*s*. 6*d*. respectively. The Prayers for the Royal Family were also altered by cancellation following the death of George II and accession of George III on 25 October 1760. The 'occasional prayers' (special services, State Holidays, etc.) were printed for only a part of the edition.‡

The second edition appeared later in 1760. It was set in English type arranged in two columns, and again two impressions were printed, with and without borders of the same ornament. It was first published at 7*s*. 6*d*., but in 1761 the price was raised to 8*s*. 6*d*. The Royal Prayers are found in the second state only, as cancels; and the 'occasional prayers' are always present.

The third and final edition was published in 1762, set in long lines of Great Primer, without borders, at 8*s*. 6*d*. The Royal Prayers are found as cancels, but in a third state which mentions Queen Charlotte, whom George III had married on 8 September 1761. The 'occasional prayers' were, as in the case of the first edition, printed for only a part of the edition.

Title-pages: There are a number of variant title-pages, which may be arranged in four Groups.

Group 1: 1760, first edition only. Four varieties: without border, 6*s*. 6*d*.; with border, 6*s*. 6*d*.; without border, 7*s*. 6*d*.; with border, 7*s*. 6*d*.

Group 2: 1760, second edition only, 7*s*. 6*d*. Two varieties: with and without border.

Group 3: 1761, first and second editions, 8*s*. 6*d*. Varieties with and without borders, but there are at least two different settings in this group.

Group 4: 1762, third edition only, 8*s*. 6*d*., without border; invariant.

The title-pages read as follows:

[Group 1] The BOOK of | Common Prayer, | *And Adminiſtration of the* | SACRAMENTS, | AND OTHER | RITES and CEREMONIES | OF THE | CHURCH, | According to the Uſe of | The CHURCH of ENGLAND: | TOGETHER WITH THE | PSALTER | OR | PSALMS of DAVID, | *Pointed as they are to be ſung or ſaid in Churches.* | [plain rule] | *CAMBRIDGE,* | Printed by JOHN BASKERVILLE, Printer to the Univerſity; | by whom they are ſold, and by B. DOD, Bookſeller, | in Ave-Mary Lane, London. M DCC LX. |

† The first issue is roughly dated by a letter which J. Benson sent to his aunt on 4 July 1760 with a copy of the first edition with borders (Group 1, 6*s*. 6*d*.), which copy, he said, was 'the second [which] has yet been bound'; both letter and prayer book now belong to Mr A. N. L. Munby.

‡ Baskerville to the Vice-Chancellor, 31 May 1759: 'I propose printing off 2000 the first impression, but only 1000 of the State holydays &c' (Straus and Dent, p. 99).

(Price Six [Seven] Shillings and Six Pence, unbound.) [Two of the four varieties within a border of 'lozenge and star' ornaments, with corner pieces, within plain rules]

[GROUP 2] [Reads as Group 1 (*7s. 6d.*) but a new setting with line 3 in roman, not italic. Some of the same type used.]

[GROUP 3] [Reads as Group 2 except for the last two lines, which read:]
in Ave-Mary Lane, London. M DCC LXI. | (*Price Eight Shillings and Six Pence, unbound.*) [There are at least two, and probably more, different settings of this page, textually identical. Plates X–XI.]

[GROUP 4] [Reads as Group 2 except for the last two lines, which read:]
in Ave-Mary Lane, London. M DCC LXII. | (Price Eight Shillings and Six Pence, unbound.) [Some of the type that was used to print Group 1 and Group 2 title-pages is found again here, notably '*CAMBRIDGE*' in the imprint, where the '*D*' is identifiable by a pinhole in the arc of the bowl. A tissue slip printed with 'lozenge and star' ornaments is sometimes found pasted over the price.]

NOTES: GROUP 1 (*7s. 6d.*) and GROUP 3 title-pages are always found as *cancellantia.*

A copy of the second edition without borders in Cambridge University Library (Tc. 77. 1) has a cancel title-page which must have been printed during the nineteenth century; it is on part of a sheet of foolscap paper (mark Pro Patria), and a number of fat-face types are used. Typographically it seems to belong to the eighteen-forties, but the paper is probably older. It bears two dates: 'MDCCLXI' and '1762'.

12 THE BOOK OF COMMON PRAYER, 8° [FIRST EDITION], 1760, 1761

INTRODUCTION AND TITLE-PAGE: See above.

FORMULA: [? Printing Royal] 8°: a–b^8 c^4 B–T^8 U^6 χ1 x–2a^8 2b^2 X–2L^8 2M^2 2N–2P^8 2Q^4 (with cancels at a2, F1, G7, R5, x1, x3, x4, y8, X5, 2L8; B8, C6, C7, D2 cancelled later) [2O3 signed '2O4'] 347 leaves, unnumbered.

Note: the first edition is often found without sections x–2b, 2N–2Q (the 'occasional prayers'), which were issued with only part of the edition. The table of contents (a3^r) remains unchanged.

CONTENTS: a1–a1^v blank, a2 title, a2^v blank, a3 The Contents, a3^v–a8^v The Preface, etc., b1–b1^v table of Proper Lessons, b2–b7^v The Calendar, b8–c4^v tables, B1–C1 Morning Prayer, C1^v–C7^v Evening Prayer, C7^v–E2^v special prayers (The Creed, The Litany, Prayers and Thanksgivings), E2^v–S7^v The Collects, Epistles and Gospels, S8–χ1^v The Communion, x1–2b2^v occasional services (three orders of Baptism, A Catechism, The Order of Confirmation, The Solemnization of Matrimony, The Visitation and Communion of the Sick, The Burial of the Dead, The Churching of Women, A Commination), X1–2L8^v Psalms, 2N1–2P4^v special forms of prayer (At Sea, Gunpowder Treason, King Charles the Martyr, The King's Restoration, The Twenty-second of June), 2P5–2Q4 Articles of Religion, 2Q4^v A Table of Kindred and Affinity.

Variants: Two impressions, one with and the other without borders.

Cancels: (1) *Cancellanda* F1, G7, R5, x1, x3, x4, y8, X5, 2L8 not seen.

(2) For cancel a2, see Title-pages, Groups 1 and 3, above.

(3) Cancels B8, C6, C7, D2. These leaves were cancelled in order to alter the prayers for the Royal Family in Morning Prayer, Evening Prayer and the Litany following the accession of George III on 25 October 1760. They may be told apart as follows:

Cancellanda: 'That it may pleaſe thee to bleſs and preſerve [etc.] their Royal Highneſſes George Prince of *Wales*, the Princeſs Dowager of *Wales*, the Duke, the Princeſſes, and all the Royal Family.'

Cancellantia: 'That it may pleaſe thee to bleſs and preſerve [etc.] her Royal Highneſs the Princeſs Dowager of *Wales*, and all the Royal Family.'

(4) The dates, etc., in the Form of Prayer for the Twenty-second of June (i.e. the accession of George II) were not altered in most copies of this edition.

(5) There is, however, a rare state—I know of only three copies—in which sections x–2b, 2N–2Q, the 'occasional prayers', are found in a new setting. The only one of these new sections that has any important textual change is 2P, which has a Form of Prayer for the Twenty-fifth of October (accession of George III), and also mentions Queen Charlotte (married to the King on 8 September 1761) and has a proclamation dated 7 October 1761. There are no cancels in the reset sections.

These reset sections are something of a puzzle, since, while they are obviously late, they occur in two of the known copies (King's College, Cambridge, Keynes Library, and Birmingham University Library) together with Group 1 (6*s*. 6*d*.) title-pages (with border), which is of course an early variety. The other copy (not seen by me, but noted by Ralph Straus) appears to have had a similar title-page, and to have had borders.

Paper: Two very similar lots of medium quality laid, no marks, no uncut copy seen, but size of sheet is at least 25 × 19½ in., so probably *Large Printing Royal.* The better of the two papers appears to be used from B to Z, not including x–2b, and the other paper for the rest of the book; but it is hard to be sure exactly where the change takes place. Baskerville wrote to the Vice-Chancellor on 31 May 1759 that 'The paper is very good and stands me in 27 or 28 shillings the ream' (Straus and Dent, p. 99). This rather high price may possibly mean that the paper was *Second Writing Super Royal* (see Philip Gaskell, 'Notes on Eighteenth-Century British Paper', *The Library*, 5th series, vol. xii (Oxford, 1957), p. 42).

Type: Text, *Great Primer*; 'occasional prayers', *Pica.* Long lines.

Notes: Published on 19 May 1760 (*Birmingham Gazette*, no. 964). For details of prices unbound, and of an early copy, see Introduction, above.

13 THE BOOK OF COMMON PRAYER, 8° [second edition], 1760, 1761

Introduction and Title-page: See pp. 30–31 above.

Formula: [? Printing Royal] 8°: a–b^8 c^4 B–P^8 Q^6 r–y^4 z^2 R–2C^8 2D^4 2E^2 2F–2K^4 2L^2 (with cancels at a1, B7, C3.6). 272 leaves, unnumbered.

Note: The 'occasional prayers' (r–z, 2F–2L) are always present.

Contents: a1 title, a1^v blank, a2 The Contents, a2^v–a7^v The Preface, etc., a8–b1^v table of Proper Lessons, b2–b7^v The Calendar, b8–c4^v tables, B1–B7 Morning Prayer, B7^v–C4 Evening Prayer, C4–D4 special prayers (The Creed, The Litany, Prayers and Thanksgivings), C4^v–P2 The

Collects, Epistles and Gospels, P2v–Q6v The Communion, r1–z2v occasional services (three orders of Baptism, A Catechism, The Order of Confirmation, The Solemnization of Matrimony, The Visitation and Communion of the Sick, The Burial of the Dead, The Churching of Women, A Commination), R1–2E2v Psalms, 2F1–2I3v special forms of prayer (At Sea, Gunpowder Treason, King Charles the Martyr, The King's Restoration, The Twenty-second of June), 2I4–2L2 Articles of Religion, 2L2v A Table of Kindred and Affinity.

VARIANTS: Two impressions, one with and the other without borders.

CANCELS: B7 and C3.6 must have been cancelled in order to alter the prayers for the Royal Family from the first to the second state (see First Edition, CANCELS (3), above), although *cancellanda* have not been seen; as in normal copies of the first edition, the Form of Prayer for the Twenty-second of June remains unaltered.

For cancel a1, see Title-pages, Groups 2 and 3, above.

PAPER: As for the first edition; the better paper seems to end here at sig. N.

TYPE: Text, *English*; 'occasional prayers', *Small Pica*. Two columns.

NOTE: Published after 25 October 1760 (state of the Royal Prayers).

14 [ROBERT DODSLEY], SELECT FABLES, 8°, 1761

TITLE-PAGE: *SELECT FABLES* | OF | ESOP | AND OTHER FABULISTS. | IN THREE BOOKS.| *—Is not the earth* | *With various living* creatures, *and the air* | *Replenifhed, and all thefe at thy command* | *To come and play before thee? Knoweft thou not* | *Their language and their Ways? They alfo know,* | *And reafon not contemptibly: with thefe* | *Find paftime.* Paradife Loft. *b.* 8. *l.* 370. | [copperplate vignette, unsigned] | *BIRMINGHAM,* | Printed by JOHN BASKERVILLE, for | R. and J. DODS LEY in Pall mall. 1761. | Price bound Five Shillings.

FORMULA: [? Post] 8°: a⁶ χ1 b–e⁸ f⁴(–f4) B–K⁸(±K3) L–P⁸ Q⁴ [E2, E3, K2, K3, P4 unsigned]. It is possible that certain whole sheets were cancelled; Shenstone wrote to Thomas Percy on 10 November 1760, mentioning 'Mistakes yt have occasioned ye Loss of three or four reams of Paper' (Williams, *Letters of Shenstone*, p. 565). Pp. [2] i–iv i–lxxviii 1–204 *205–32* (for errors, see below).

CONTENTS: a1 title, a1v blank, a2–a3 Preface, a3v blank, ²i sub-title to the Life, ²ii blank, ²iii–liii The Life of Esop, liv blank, lv sub-title to the Essay, lvi blank, lvii–lxxviii An Essay on Fable, 1–204 Fables, Ancient, Modern and Original (pp. 2, 62, 64, 132 blank), *205–32* Index.

CANCEL: K3 *cancellandum* not seen.

ERRORS: Misnumeration: main roman series runs i–vii vii–xxxix xli–lxxviii (=lxxviii); arabic series runs 1–130 *131–3* 133–75 177–204 *205–32* (=232). Points missing in the headlines of pp. 20, 25, 55, 77, 93, 98, 113, 116 (sometimes), 145 and 182.

PLATES: Copperplates printed on title-page and on pp. 3, 61, 65, 130, ¹133, 204 (those on pp. 61 and 204 signed Wale and Grignion); also frontispiece, and plates facing B2, C1v, C7, D5v, E4v, F1, F8v, G7v, H7, I6v, K3, L3, M4, N4, O3v (unsigned).

Note: In Lord Rothschild's copy the inserted plates have been removed, and some of the other plates given pen and wash frames (*The Rothschild Library* (Cambridge, privately printed, 1954), vol. I, p. 193).

PAPER: Good quality wove: watermark, a 'W' on the edge of the sheet (see James Wardrop, 'Mr. Whatman, Papermaker', *Signature*, 1st series, no. 9 (London, 1938), 7); no uncut copy seen, but size of sheet is at least 19 × 14½ in., so probably *Post*. Plates: a slightly heavier wove, no mark.

TYPE: Text, *Long Primer* leaded; Life, *Pica*; Preface, *Small Pica*.

NOTES: Shenstone to Thomas Percy, 11 August 1760: '*Dodsley*...resides here [i.e. at The Leasowes] for near two months, to correct y[e] edition of Fables begun by Baskerville' (Williams, *Letters of Shenstone*, p. 559).

Shenstone to Percy, early 1761: 'I procured a copy of the Fables from M[r] Baskerville, *before* the Cuts *were inserted*' (Williams, *op. cit.* p. 568). This copy, with Shenstone's own wash drawings instead of the copperplate decorations, has survived, and was sold to Birmingham University Library at Sotheby's on 23 July 1956; the catalogue contains a plate showing some of Shenstone's work.

Birmingham Gazette, no. 1003: *Select Fables* published on about 9 February 1761, price 5*s*. bound.

Shenstone to Richard Graves, 2 May 1761: 'Mr. Dodsley had sold two thousand of his Fables long ago; but complained that he should *lose* thirty pounds by my neighbour Baskerville's impression; and that he should not be more than ten pounds gainer, upon the *whole*' (Williams, *op. cit.* p. 578).

Shenstone to Percy, October 1761: 'I fancy Dodsley thinks of causing Baskerville very soon to print a new Edition of his Fables' (Williams, *op. cit.* p. 603). The new edition did not in fact appear until 1764 (see no. 27 below).

Plate XII (Shenstone's copy).

15 JUVENAL AND PERSIUS, *SATYRAE*, 4°, 1761

TITLE-PAGE: D. JUNII | JUVENALIS | ET | AULI | PERSII FLACCI | SATYRAE. | *BIRMINGHAMIAE:* | Typis JOHANNIS BASKER VILLE. | M DCC LXI.

FORMULA: Printing Royal 4°: *A*[4] B–2G[4] (with cancels at E2, K4, U4, Z3). Pp. 1–240.

CONTENTS: 1 title, 2 blank, 3 sub-title to Juvenal, 4 blank, 5–199 Juvenalis Satyrae I–XVI (pp. 14, 38, 56, 88, 114, 140, 158 and 196 blank), 200 blank, 201 sub-title to Persius, 202 blank, 203–40 Persii Satyrae I–VI (pp. 212, 226 and 236 blank).

CANCELS: E2: *-andum*, p. 35 l. 14 '...cafus in improvidus...'; *-ans*, '...cafus improvidus...'
K4: *-andum*, p. 79 l. 12 '...quare cinnus?...'; *-ans*, '...quare cincinnus?...'
U4: *-andum*, p. 160 l. 18 [omitted]; *-ans* [present; begins] 'Quos habeat...'
Z3: No textual difference between *cancellandum* and *cancellans*, nor any other obvious reason for cancellation. They may easily be distinguished by the paper; the *cancellans* is of course reset.

ERRORS: Headlines: p. 48, 'IV.' for 'V.'; p. 67, 'IV.' for 'VI.'; pp. 84, 85, 'VII.' for 'VI.', the second 'I' and the point scraped out and a new point stamped in.

PAPER: Two lots. *A*–2D: good quality *Printing Royal* laid, no marks, size of sheet 24½ × 19 in. 2E–2G and *cancellantia*: medium quality *Printing Royal* laid, no marks, same size, now stained badly in purplish patches (the poorer paper found only in 2F and *cancellantia* in some copies).

TYPE: Text, *Great Primer* leaded.

NOTES: Published on about 4 May 1761, price 12*s*. in sheets (*Birmingham Gazette*, no. 1015. In the Proposals for the Bible of 1759 and 1760 (no. viii above), there is an advance notice of *Juvenal and Persius* at 16*s*. in sheets.). 250 copies remained in 1775 (pp. xvii–xviii above).

16 WILLIAM CONGREVE, WORKS, 3 VOLUMES, 8°, 1761

TITLE-PAGE: [General] THE | WORKS | OF | Mr. *WILLIAM CONGREVE.* | IN THREE VOLUMES. | CONSISTING OF | His PLAYS and POEMS. | [rule of 'lozenge and star' ornaments] | *BIRMINGHAM,* | Printed by JOHN BASKERVILLE; | For J. and R. TONSON, in the *Strand, London.* | M DCC LXI.

[Volume] THE | WORKS | OF | Mr. *WILLIAM CONGREVE.* | VOLUME THE FIRST [SECOND] [THIRD]. | CONTAINING, | *The* OLD BATCHELOR, *a Comedy.* | *The* DOUBLE DEALER, *a Comedy.* [LOVE *for* LOVE, *a Comedy.* | *The* WAY *of the* WORLD, *a Comedy.*] [*The* MOURNING BRIDE, *a Tragedy.* | *The Judgment of* PARIS, *a Maſque.* | SEMELE, *an Opera.* | POEMS *upon ſeveral* OCCASIONS.] | [rule of 'lozenge and star' ornaments] | *BIRMINGHAM,* | Printed by JOHN BASKERVILLE; | For J. and R. TONSON, in the *Strand, London.* | M DCC LXI.

Note: The invariant parts of the volume titles are all printed from the same setting of type, with the necessary alterations of spacing. The general title is from a different setting.

FORMULAE: Writing or Printing Royal 8°:

Vol. I: A^4 a–b^8 B–Z^8 $2A^4$ (with sigs. *A*, a and b cancelled) [b 1 unsigned]. Pp. i–xl 1–360.

Vol. II: A^2 a^4 B–$2I^8$ $2K^2$. Pp. [1–12] 17–516 (=512).

Vol. III: A^2 a^4 B–$2I^8$ $2K^2$ (2H3 possibly a cancel) [the volume signature ('VOL. III.') has been printed as 'VOL. II.' on B1, C1 and D1; the extra 'I' has been stamped in over the second point]. Pp. [1–12] 17–516 (=512).

CONTENTS:

Vol. I: i general title, ii blank, iii volume title, iv blank, v–viii Preface, ix–xxiv The Life of Congreve, xxv sub-title to The Old Batchelor, xxvi blank, xxvii–xxx Dedication, xxxi–xxxv poems by Southerne, Marsh and Higgons, xxxvi–xxxix Prologues, xl Dramatis Personæ, 1–164 The Old Batchelor, 165–6 Epilogue, 167 sub-title to The Double Dealer, 168 blank, 169–78 The Epistle Dedicatory, 179–83 poem by Dryden, 184–5 Prologue, 186 Dramatis Personæ, 187–358 The Double Dealer, 359–60 Epilogue.

Vol. II: *A*1 volume title, *A*1ᵛ blank, *A*2 sub-title to Love for Love, *A*2ᵛ blank, a1–a2ᵛ Dedication, a3–a4 Prologue, a4ᵛ Dramatis Personæ, 17–274 Love for Love, 275–7 Epilogue, 278 blank, 279 sub-title to The Way of the World, 280 blank, 281–8 Dedication, 289–91 poem by Steele, 292–3 Prologue, 294 Dramatis Personæ, 295–514 The Way of the World, 515–16 Epilogue.

Vol. III: *A*1 volume title, *A*1ᵛ blank, *A*2 sub-title to The Mourning Bride, *A*2ᵛ blank, a1–a2ᵛ The Epistle Dedicatory, a3–a4 Prologue, a4ᵛ Dramatis Personæ, 17–151 The Mourning Bride, 152–3 Epilogue, 154 blank, 155 sub-title to The Judgment of Paris, 156 blank, 157–66 The Judgment of Paris, 167 sub-title to Semele, 168 blank, 169–71 Argument, 172 Persons Represented, 173–217 Semele, 218 blank, 219 sub-title to Poems, 220 blank, 221–3 Epistle, 224 blank, 225–492 Poems upon several Occasions (p. 428 blank), 493 sub-title to Humor in Comedy, 494 blank, 495–514 Concerning Humor in Comedy, 515–16 A Table of the Poems, &c.

CANCELS: Vol. I. The cancellation of *A*–b may have been on account of the very poor quality of the paper on which these sections were originally printed; the textual changes were inconsiderable. The chief differences are as follows:

*A*3v: *-andum*, penultimate line 'defective-'; *-ans*, 'defective.'
a1v: *-andum*, l. 12 '*Kilkenney*'; *-ans*, '*Kilkenny*'
a8r: *-andum*, l. 6 'in Sate'; *-ans*, 'in State'
b3v: *-andum*, l. 1 'Cenſures'; *-ans*, 'Cenſurers'
b8v: *-andum*, l. 3 'pretending'; *-ans*, 'pre-'

Vol. III. 2H3 also exists in another state, with (p. 485, l. 19) 'ſhall know End.' for 'ſhall know no End.'† I have not seen this state; and, since in the copies seen neither 2H3 nor 2H3.6 appears to be a *cancellans*, this may be another case of the cancellation of a whole section.

ERRORS: Vol. III, p. 27, headline lacks point.

PLATES: Vol. I: plates facing *A*1, B1, M4.
Vol. II: plates facing B1, S4.
Vol. III: plate facing *A*1.
(All signed Hayman and Grignion, except frontispiece (vol. I, facing *A*1) which is signed Kneller and Chambars.) The plates are sometimes placed elsewhere.

PAPER: Three lots of *Writing* or *Printing Royal* laid: (*a*) Vol. I *cancellanda*: very poor quality, no marks, now purplish and crumbly. (*b*) Vol. I *cancellantia*: poor quality, no marks, now foxed: similar to the poorer paper of no. 15. (*c*) Medium quality, marks Strasbourg bend/LVG. No uncut copy seen, but size of sheet is at least 23 × 18½ in.

TYPE: Text, *English*, solid and leaded; Preface, *Great Primer* leaded; heavy use of 'lozenge and star' ornaments throughout.

NOTES: A *Catalogue des Livres en Feuilles des Libraires Associés de Paris* ([Paris, *c.* 1804], p. 100) has the following entry: 'Congreve's works, 3 vol. in 8 Baskerville fig. 60f.'‡ This suggests that the book was remaindered. There are no other Baskervilles listed in this catalogue.

17 JOSEPH ADDISON, WORKS, 4 VOLUMES, 4°, 1761

TITLE-PAGE: [Vol. I] THE | WORKS | OF THE LATE | RIGHT HONOR ABLE | *JOSEPH ADDISON*, Eſq; | [rule of 'lozenge and star' ornaments beneath plain rule] | VOLUME the FIRST. | [rule of 'lozenge and star' ornaments] | With a Complete INDEX. | [rule of 'lozenge and star' ornaments over plain rule] | *BIRMINGHAM:* | Printed by JOHN BASKERVILLE, for J. and R. TONSON, | At *Shakeſpear's Head* in the *Strand*, LONDON. | M DCC LXI.

[Vols. II, III and IV: from essentially the same setting of type, with slight changes of spacing, and the following textual alterations: l. 6, the words 'SECOND', 'THIRD' and 'FOURTH' respectively for 'FIRST'. Penultimate line, full stop after '*Strand*', 'LONDON' deleted.]

† Townsend and Currier, *op. cit.* (p. 20 above), p. 292.
‡ The rate of exchange was about 25f. to the pound sterling in 1804 (*The Star, The Times*), which means that 60f. was worth about £2. 8*s*.

FORMULAE: [? Printing] Royal 4°:

Vol. I: a–c⁴ d² B–3Z⁴ ²3H–3Z⁴ [¹3Z2 unsigned]. Pp. i–xxviii 1–538 [2] 413–544 (=674).

Vol. II: *A*⁴ B–4A⁴(–4A4) [2P1 signed 'pP']. Pp. [1–8] 1–550.

Vol. III: A–4E⁴. Pp. 1–592.

Vol. IV: A–4B⁴. Pp. 1–568.

CONTENTS:

Vol. I: i title, ii blank, iii–v dedication, vi blank, vii–xx The Preface, xxi–xxv poem by Tickell, xxvi–xxvii The Contents, xxviii blank, 1–501 Poems on Several Occasions (including Rosamond, Cato and The Drummer; pp. 2, 6, 60, 78, 80, 248 and 378 blank), 502 blank, 503–37 Poemata (p. 504 blank), 538 blank, ¹3Z2 blank, ¹3Z2ᵛ 'Directions to the Binder. This leaf is to be cut out...' (and is therefore frequently missing), ²413–537 Dialogues upon the Usefulness of Ancient Medals (pp. ²414, 418, 518, 520, 524, 526, 530, 532 and 536 blank), ²538 blank, 539–42 Index, 543–4 blank.

Vol. II: *A*1 title, *A*1ᵛ blank, *A*2 sub-title to Remarks on Several Parts of Italy, *A*2ᵛ blank, *A*3–*A*3ᵛ dedication, *A*4–*A*4ᵛ Preface, 1–171 (Remarks on Several Parts, etc.; headlines vary), 172 blank, 173–372 The Tatler (p. 174 blank), 373–538 The Spectator (to no. 89, p. 374 blank), 539–49 Index, 550 blank.

Vol. III: 1 title, 2 blank, 3–579 The Spectator (nos. 90–505), 580 blank, 581–91 Index, 592 blank.

Vol. IV: 1 title, 2 blank, 3–117 The Spectator (nos. 507–600), 118 blank, 119–271 The Guardian (p. 120 blank), 272–8 The Lover, 279–300 The Present State of the War (p. 280 blank), 301–7 The Trial of Count Tariff (p. 302 blank), 308 blank, 309–32 The Whig-examiner (p. 310 blank), 333–522 The Free Holder (p. 334 blank), 523–55 Of the Christian Religion (p. 524 blank), 556 blank, 557–66 Index, 567–8 blank.

ERRORS: Misnumeration: vol. I, main series, 1–538 [2] 413–544 (=674); '525' for ²537. Vol. II, '125' for 135, '171' for 271, '28' for 285, '254' for 354; occasionally '37' for 371. Vol. III, '213' for 218. Vol. IV, occasionally '52' for 527.

Other errors: Vol. II, 260, periodical number '246' for 146; 212, occasionally, page number and periodical number transposed. Vol. III, no point in headline on pp. 41, 148, 163, 230, 236, 256, 288, 300, 314, 340, 488; 179, point after page number. Vol. IV, no point in headline on pp. 23, 49, 83, 93.

(There were also changes made during the run to the rules of ornaments in vol. III, title-page and p. 3, and vol IV, pp. 82, 301, 303.)

PLATES: Vol. I, frontispiece (signed Kneller and Miller) and three plates (signed Hayman and Grignion), facing a1, L4, 2I4, 3C1. Vol. II, seven leaves of cuts, facing G1ᵛ, G4, L1, M3ᵛ, O1, O4ᵛ, S4ᵛ. (There are also cuts in vol. I on pp. ²523, ²525, ²529, ²531, ²535, ²537.) The cuts in vol. II are unlikely to have been printed by Baskerville, since the leaves have directions printed on them in a non-Baskerville roman, probably Caslon.

PAPER: Medium quality laid, marks Strasbourg bend/LVG, no uncut copy seen but size of sheet is at least 23¾ × 19 in.; probably *Printing Royal*. The cuts in vol. II on a similar paper, but countermark GR.

TYPE: Text, *Great Primer* leaded and solid, *English*; Dedication, *Double Pica* leaded; Index, *Long Primer*. Vol. I, p. 517, Baskerville's two-line *Double Pica* Greek caps; p. 516 and Vol. II, p. 137, Baskerville's *Great Primer* Greek. Vol. II, p. 1, 'arabesque' ornaments.

18 ANON., AN ODE UPON THE FLEET, 4°, 1761

TITLE-PAGE: AN | ODE | UPON THE | FLEET and ROYAL YATCH [*sic*], | GOING TO CONDUCT | *The* Princeſs *of MECKLENBURG* | TO BE | QUEEN | OF | GREAT BRITAIN. | [rule of 'lozenge and star' ornaments; a high space under the sixth unit from the right] | *BIRMINGHAM:* | Printed by JOHN BASKERVILLE, and ſold by | *R.* and *J. Dodſley, M. Cooper &c.* | M DCC LXI.

FORMULA: Crown 4°: A^2 χ1 B^4. Pp. 1–14.

CONTENTS: 1 title, 2 blank, 3–13 An Ode on the Royal Nuptials, 14 blank.

PAPER: Medium quality *Crown* laid, no marks, size of sheet 20 × 15 in.

TYPE: Text, *Great Primer* leaded.

NOTES: Published by September, 1761 (*The Monthly Review*, vol. XXV, p. 229).

Shenstone to Richard Graves, 14 September 1761: 'Last night was brought me, from Baskerville's press...very *pompously* printed, the most despicable Grub-street I ever saw' (Williams, *Letters of Shenstone*, p. 588).

19 THE BOOK OF COMMON PRAYER, 8° [THIRD EDITION], 1762

INTRODUCTION AND TITLE-PAGE: See pp. 30–31 above.

FORMULA: [? Printing Royal] 8°: a–b^8 c^4 B–$2S^8$ $2T^4$ (with cancels at a2, B8, C6, D3). 344 leaves, unnumbered.

Note: The third edition sometimes lacks the 'occasional prayers', i.e. U7 to 2A7 inclusive and 2Q to 2T inclusive.

CONTENTS: a1 title, a1v blank, a2 The Contents, a2v–a7v The Preface, etc., a8–b1v table of Proper Lessons, b2–b7v The Calendar, b8–c4v tables, B1–C1 Morning Prayer, C1v–E2v special prayers (The Creed, The Litany, Prayers and Thanksgivings), E3–S6v The Collects, Epistles and Gospels, S7–U6v The Communion, U7–2A7v occasional services (three orders of Baptism, A Catechism, The Order of Confirmation, The Solemnization of Matrimony, The Visitation and Communion of the Sick, The Burial of the Dead, The Churching of Women, A Commination), 2A8–2P8v Psalms, 2Q1–2S4v special forms of prayer (At Sea, Gunpowder Treason, King Charles the Martyr, The King's Restoration, The Twenty-fifth of October), 2S5–2T4 Articles of Religion, 2T4v A Table of Kindred and Affinity.

CANCELS: *Cancellanda* a2 (the Contents and beginning of Preface), B8, C6 and D3 not seen.

The prayers for the Royal Family are in a third state on *cancellantia* B8, C6 and D3, reading: 'That it may pleaſe thee to bleſs and preſerve [etc.] our gracious Queen CHARLOTTE, her Royal Highneſs the Princeſs Dowager of *Wales*, and all the Royal Family.'

The Queen's name is included in the (uncancelled) Form of Prayer for the Twenty-fifth of October.

PAPER: Medium quality laid, no marks, similar to the papers used for the first and second editions.

TYPE: As in the first edition (reset). Long lines.

NOTE: Published on about 15 February 1762 (*Birmingham Gazette*, no. 1056).

20 THE BOOK OF COMMON PRAYER, 12°, 1762

TITLE-PAGE: [*Cancellandum*] The BOOK of | *COMMON PRAYER*, | And Adminiſtration of the | SACRAMENTS, | AND OTHER | RITES and CEREMONIES | OF THE | CHURCH, | According to the Uſe of | The CHURCH of ENGLAND: | Together with the | PSALTER | OR | PSALMS of DAVID, | *Pointed as they are to be ſung or ſaid in Churches.* | [plain double rule] | *CAMBRIDGE,* | Printed by J. BASKERVILLE, Printer to the Univerſity, by | whom they are ſold in Cambridge, and by B. DOD, | Bookſeller, in Ave-Mary Lane, London. 1762. | *Price Four Shillings and Sixpence unbound.*

[*Cancellans* is largely reset, reading as above except line 2, 'Common Prayer,'; last line, '(*Price Five Shillings, unbound.*)'.]

FORMULA: [? Writing Medium] 12° in sixes: a⁶(± a2) b–c⁶ B–2H⁶ [a3 signed 'a2'; C2 unsigned]. 198 leaves, unnumbered.

CONTENTS: a1–a1ᵛ blank, a2 title, a2ᵛ blank, a3 (signed 'a2') The Contents, a3ᵛ–a6 The Preface, etc., a6ᵛ–b1 table of Proper Lessons, b1ᵛ–c1 The Calendar, c1ᵛ–c6 tables, c6ᵛ blank, B1–B5 Morning Prayer, B5ᵛ–C2 Evening Prayer, C2ᵛ–D1ᵛ special prayers (The Creed, The Litany, Prayers and Thanksgivings), D2–N2ᵛ The Collects, Epistles and Gospels, N3–O5 The Communion, O5ᵛ–S6ᵛ occasional services (three orders of Baptism, A Catechism, The Order of Confirmation, The Solemnization of Matrimony, The Visitation and Communion of the Sick, The Burial of the Dead, The Churching of Women, A Commination), T1–2E2ᵛ Psalms, 2E3–2G5ᵛ special forms of prayer (At Sea, Gunpowder Treason, King Charles the Martyr, The King's Restoration, The Twenty Fifth of October), 2G6–2H6 Articles of Religion, 2H6ᵛ A Table of Kindred and Affinity.

CANCEL: See Title-page, above. The *cancellans* title-page, which is much commoner than the *cancellandum*, occasionally has a tissue slip printed with 'lozenge and star' ornaments pasted over the bottom line (i.e. the price).

ERRORS: D6ʳ, R5ʳ: no point in headlines.

PAPER: Thin, medium quality laid, marks Fleur-de-lys in a shield crowned over LVG/IV; no uncut copy seen, but size of sheet at least 20½ × 16¼ in., so probably *Writing Medium.*

TYPE: Text, *Brevier No. 1*; Preface, *Nonpareil.*

NOTES: The text of the Royal Prayers, etc., is the same as that of the third edition octavo Prayer Book (no. 19 above).

Published in April 1762, price 4*s.* 6*d.* in sheets (*Birmingham Gazette*, no. 1056). Baskerville agreed with the University to print an edition of 4000 copies (Straus and Dent, p. 112).

21 STERNHOLD AND HOPKINS, PSALMS, 12°, 1762

TITLE-PAGE: THE | WHOLE BOOK | OF | PSALMS, | Collected into | Engliſh Metre, | BY | *Thomas Sternhold, John Hopkins,* | and Others. | Set forth and allowed to be Sung in all Churches, | of all the People together, before and after Morn-|ing and Evening Prayer; and alſo before and | after Sermon; and moreover in private Houſes, | for their Godly Solace and Comfort: laying | apart all ungodly Songs and Ballads, which tend | only to the nouriſhing of Vice, and corrupting | of Youth. | [plain rule] | *If any be afflicted, let him pray; and if any be merry, let | him ſing Pſalms.* James v. 13. | *Let the Word of God dwell plenteouſly in you, in all Wiſ-|dom, teaching and exhorting one another in Pſalms, | Hymns, and Spiritual Songs, ſinging unto the Lord | with Grace in your Hearts.* Coloff. iii. 16. | [plain double rule] | (By Permiſſion of the Stationer's Company.) | *BIRMINGHAM,* | Printed by JOHN BASKERVILLE, 1762. | (*Price One Shilling and Sixpence in Sheets.*)

FORMULA: [? Writing Medium] 12° in sixes: A^2 B–L^6(–L6). 61 leaves, unnumbered.

CONTENTS: A 1 title, A 1ᵛ blank, A 2–A 2ᵛ An Alphabetical Table, B 1–L 2 Psalms I–CL, L 2ᵛ blank, L 3–L 5ᵛ Veni Creator, etc., L 5ᵛ Gloria Patri.

ERROR: G 2ʳ: no point in headline.

PAPER: As no. 20.

TYPE: Text, *Nonpareil.*

22 BRADY AND TATE, PSALMS, 12°, 1762

TITLE-PAGE: A New Verſion | OF THE | PSALMS | OF | *DAVID,* | Fitted to the TUNES uſed in | CHURCHES. | [plain rule] | BY | *N. BRADY,* D.D. Chaplain in Ordinary, | and *N. TATE,* Eſq; Poet-Laureat to His | Majeſty. | [plain double rule] | (With Permiſſion of the Stationer's Company.) | *BIR MINGHAM,* | Printed by JOHN BASKERVILLE, 1762. | (*Price One Shilling and Sixpence in Sheets.*)

FORMULA: [? Writing Medium] 12° in sixes: A^2 χ1 B–C^6(±C3) D–I^6 K1 [E3 signed 'E2']. 52 leaves, unnumbered.

CONTENTS: A 1 title, A 1ᵛ blank, A 2 the Bishop of London's imprimatur, A 2ᵛ–χ1 An Alphabetical Table, χ1ᵛ Directions about the Tunes and Measures, B 1–K 1 Psalms I–CL, K 1ᵛ Gloria Patri, &c.

CANCEL: *Cancellandum* C 3 not seen.

ERROR: D 6ʳ headline has extra comma.

PAPER: As no. 20.

TYPE: Text, *Nonpareil*; 'Directions', *Long Primer.*

23 HORACE, [WORKS], 12°, 1762

TITLE-PAGE: QUINTUS | HORATIUS | FLACCUS. | [copperplate vignette, signed S. Wale, C. Grignion] | *BIRMINGHAMIÆ;* | Typis *JOANNIS BASKERVILLE.* | M DCC LXII.

Formula: Post 12° in sixes: *A*1 χ^2 B–C[6] D1 D2.3 *D[2](*D2+χ1) E–2C[6] 2*D*[2] (with cancels at B1, H1, L2, M1, M5, N2, P5, Q4, R4, T2 and T6; frontispiece facing *A*1). Pp. [8] 1–300 *301–4*.

Note: Although it would appear from this formula that the book is fairly straightforward, apart from sections D and *D, the papers on which it is printed show that it must have been printed or gathered, or both, in a most unusual way.

Three sorts of paper are used, which I have called (*a*), (*b*) and (*c*) (see the section on Paper below for their characteristics). One would expect that, except where there are cancels or other obvious abnormalities, each section would be printed on one sort of paper only. This is not the case. Conjugate pairs of leaves (that is $1.6, $2.5 and $3.4) are on different sorts of paper within the section; usually two sorts, but occasionally each of the three pairs is on a different paper. For example, in the copy in the Keynes Bequest at King's College Library, Cambridge, Z1.6 and 3.4 are on paper (*a*), but Z2.5 is on paper (*b*). If this were the only section in which such a thing occurred it might be thought that Z2.5 were *cancellantia*, which, it so happened, could be printed together; but the fact is that all the sections from E to Z are similarly monstrous.† What is more, the distribution of paper to the parts of the sections is not consistent through the edition, nor is it to individual cancels. Let us look at how the paper is arranged in fifteen copies of sig. E. Five copies have E1.6 3.4 on (*c*), 2.5 on (*a*); four copies have E[6] on (*c*); three copies have E2.5 3.4 on (*c*), 1.6 on (*a*); one copy has E1.6 2.5 on (*a*), 3.4 on (*b*); one copy has E2.5 3.4 on (*c*), 1.6 on (*b*); and one copy has E1.6 on (*b*), 2.5 on (*a*), 3.4 on (*c*). Here is one duodecimo half sheet that can be found on one sort of paper, or two, or three, arranged in six different ways.

Contents: *A*1 title, *A*1v blank, χ1 dedication, χ1v blank, χ2 sub-title to Carmina, χ2v blank, 1–116 Carminum Lib. i–iv, 117 sub-title to Epodoi, 118 blank, 119–142 Epodon Liber, 143–5 Carmen Seculare, 146 blank, 147 sub-title to Sermones, 148 blank, 149–225 Sermonum Lib. i–ii, Sat. i–x, i–viii, 226 blank, 227 sub-title to Epistolae, 228 blank, 229–84 Epistolarum Lib. i–ii, 285–300 Ars Poetica (verso headlines, pp. 2–300, Q. Horatii), 2*D*1 blank, 2*D*1v Erratum, 2*D*2 advertisement for books printed and sold by John Baskerville, 2*D*2v blank.

Cancels: *Cancellanda* H1, L2, M1, M5, N2, Q4, R4, and T2 not seen. The principal variants of the remainder are:

B1: *-andum*, p. 1 l. 12 of text 'Agros;'; *-ans*, 'Agros,'
-andum, p. 2 heading 'AD AUG. CÆSAREM. ODE II.'; *-ans*, 'AD AUGUSTUM. ODE II.'
-andum, p. 2 l. 4 from bottom 'columbis'; *-ans*, 'palumbis'

P5: *-andum*, p. 166 l. 1: 'Non recito cuiquam, nifi...'; *-ans*, 'Neu recitem quidquam, nifi...'

T6: *-andum*, p. 215 l. 6 'Quid vis, infane, et quas res agis ? improbus'; *-ans*, 'Quid tibi vis, quas res agis, infane ? improbus'
-andum, p. 215 l. 8 'obftat'; *-ans*, 'obftet'
-andum, p. 215 l. 3 from bottom 'Frigidus a'; *-ans*, 'Frigidus e'
-andum, p. 216 l. 17 'proprium vefcor', l. 18 'Pafco libatis'; *-ans*, 'vefcor proprium', 'Libatis pafco'

Errors: Misnumeration '119' for 219 in most copies. Headlines: p. 38 '*HORAITI*'; p. 47 'LIB II.' for 'LIB. II.'.

Plates: Copperplate vignettes on the title-page (see above) and χ1 (unsigned). Frontispiece signed S. Wale, C. Grignion.

Paper: Three sorts of *Post* paper; size of sheet at least 19¼ × 14¾ in.

(*a*) Poor quality, chain 12½ mm., no watermark, badly foxed.

† The preliminaries and 2*D* are on (*b*), 2A–2C on (*a*), and B–C usually on (*a*).

(*b*) Good quality, chain 12½ mm., no watermark, unfoxed except by offset from (*a*).

(*c*) Poor quality, chain 24 mm., Post-horn watermark similar to Heawood 2741 (with the mouth of the horn to the right), slightly foxed.

It may be that papers (*a*) and (*c*) were as expensive as (*b*), and so not technically of poorer quality; but I have so described them because they have stood the passage of time less well. They are both rather lighter in weight than (*b*).

For the distribution of these papers, see the Note on FORMULA, above.

TYPE: Text, *Bourgeois*; headings and headlines, *Long Primer*.

VARIANTS: A copy in Cambridge University Library (Ff. 18. 117) has, instead of the copperplates on *A*1 and χ1, pen and wash drawings in a style very much like Wale's. The subject on the title-page is a crossed lyre and horn, smaller than the plate and an improvement upon it.† The Bute arms on χ1 are surmounted by a helm and crest instead of a coronet, and lack the motto of the Thistle, which was included in the copperplate.‡ *A*1 and χ1 are printed from the same type as that used for the standard issue, but quite differently spaced, on paper (*b*). There are a number of MS. corrections in the text. On the whole the evidence suggests that this was a trial copy for a projected second edition or issue, made in the middle of 1762.

A copy belonging to Mr James Mosley of the St Bride Foundation incorporates another experiment: the title-page is printed from the same type as usual, but with lines 2, 4 and 6 in red. This is the only known example of such decoration in the whole of Baskerville's work. The rest of this copy is also peculiar. Sections χ, B, C and P are printed from the normal 1762 setting on papers (*a*), (*b*) and (*c*); but sections D–O and Q–2C are from Sarah Baskerville's Demy 18° *Horace* of 1777.

There is a similar monstrosity at the British Museum: 1349. b. 11 has the frontispiece and preliminaries (*A*1–χ2) of the Post 12° edition of 1762 bound up with B–2C of the Demy 18° of 1777.

NOTES: Shenstone's letters of 1761–2 are full of information about the preparation and publication of this book.§ In brief, the scheme was under consideration by February 1761, and Baskerville produced a specimen of the book in June of the same year. Printing was almost finished by October 1761, but trouble with the engravers held up publication until it was published on about 31 May 1762, price 5*s*. in sheets (*Birmingham Gazette*, no. 1071). The editor was J. Livie, who later edited Baskerville's 8° *Virgil* of 1766.

24 RICHARD GARDINER, EXPEDITION TO THE WEST INDIES, THIRD EDITION, 4°, 1762

TITLE-PAGE: AN | ACCOUNT | OF THE | EXPEDITION | TO THE | *WEST INDIES*, | AGAINST | MARTINICO, | With the REDUCTION of | GUADELUPE, | And other the [*sic*] LEEWARD ISLANDS; | Subject to the *French* King, 1759. | [plain rule] | By Captain *GARDINER* of the King's *Royal Musqueteers*, | late Captain of Marines on Board his Majesty's Ship *RIPPON*,

† This title-page is reproduced in *The Book Collector*, vol. 1 (London, 1953), p. 158.

‡ Bute resigned the Thistle so that he might accept the Garter, probably soon after 27 May 1762 and before 22 September 1762; during this period he was a member of neither Order.

§ See especially Williams, *Letters of Shenstone*, pp. 569–70, 580–81, 583, 592, 595–6, 602, 619, 624, 629 and 637; and Bennett, vol. 1, pp. 118–25.

employed | on this Expedition. | [plain rule] | *Verſas ad Littora Puppes* | *Reſpiciunt, totumque allabi claſſibus Æquor.* VIRG. | *Imperî* | *Porrecta Majeſtas*, ab Ortu | *Solis* ad Heſperium Cubile | *Cuſtode Rerum CÆSARE.*—HOR. | [plain rule] | The THIRD EDITION. | [plain rule] | *BIRMINGHAM*, | Printed by *JOHN BASKERVILLE*, For *G. STEIDEL*, at the *Crown* and | *Bible*, *Maddox-Street*, *Hanover-Square*, *London.* 1762.

FORMULA: Printing Demy 4°: *A*⁴ B–M⁴ N² [C3 signed]. Pp. [6] 1–92.

CONTENTS: *A*1–*A*1ᵛ blank, *A*2 half-title, *A*2ᵛ blank, *A*3 title, *A*3ᵛ blank, *A*4–*A*4ᵛ Dedication, 1–91 text (no headlines), 92 Errata.

CANCELS: Although C3 is a line shorter than the other pages, and is unnecessarily signed, it is not a cancel.

PLATES: Four copperplates, unsigned, usually gathered at the end (printed on a *Writing Royal* laid paper in both issues).

PAPER: Two lots of *Printing Demy* laid:
(*a*) Sigs. B–M: medium quality, watermark fleur-de-lys/IV.
(*b*) Sigs. *A*, N: medium quality, no marks.
Size of sheet *c.* 21½ × 17 in.

VARIANT: Issue in Writing Royal Quarto. Paper, good quality *Writing Royal* laid, watermark Strasbourg bend/LVG, size 24¼ × 19¼ in.

TYPE: Text, *English* leaded; footnotes, *Long Primer*; Dedication, *Great Primer* leaded.

NOTE: Normally bound up with no. 25. First edition: 4°, London, 1759.

25 RICHARD GARDINER, L'EXPÉDITION AUX INDES OCCIDENTALES, 'TROISIÈME ÉDITION', 4°, 1762

TITLE-PAGE: RELATION | DE | L'EXPEDITION | AUX | *INDES OCCI DENTALES*, | CONTRE | LA MARTINIQUE, | Avec la REDUCTION de la | GUADELUPE, | Et autres ISLES ſous Vent, | Appartenant au Roi de *France*, en 1759. | [plain rule] | Par Monſ. *GARDINER* Capitaine des *Mouſ quetaires Royaux* | de S.M. Autrefois Capitaine des Troupes de Marine à bord le *RIPPON*, | Vaiſſeau de S.M. employé à cette Expedition. | [plain rule] | *Verſas ad Littora Puppes* | *Reſpiciunt, totumque allabi claſſibus Æquor.* VIRG. | *Imperî* | *Porrecta Majeſtas*, ab Ortu | *Solis* ad Heſperium Cubile | *Cuſtode Rerum CÆSARE.*—HOR. | [plain rule] | TROISIEME EDITION. | [plain rule] | *À BIRMINGHAM*, | Imprimé par *JEAN BASKERVILLE*, pour *G. STEIDEL*, à l'enſeigne de | la *Couronne* et de la *Bible*, en *Maddox-Street*, au *Quarré*, d'*Honover* [*sic*], à *Londres*, 1762.

FORMULA: Printing Demy 4°: π^4 A–L⁴M² [A3 signed]. Pp. [8] 1–92.

CONTENTS: π1–π1ᵛ blank, π2 half-title, π2ᵛ blank, π3 title, π3ᵛ blank, π4–π4ᵛ La Dédicace, 1–91 text (no headlines), 92 blank.

PLATES: This book is normally bound up with the English version, sharing the same set of plates.

PAPER: Four lots of *Printing Demy* laid:

(*a*) Sigs. A–B, D–E, G–I, L, π: as no. 24 paper (*a*).
(*b*) Sigs. C, F: as no. 24 paper (*b*).
(*c*) Sig. K: poor quality, watermark fleur-de-lys/IV.
(*d*) Sig. M: poor quality, no marks.
Size of sheet *c*. 21½ × 17 in.

VARIANT: Issue in Writing Royal 4°. Paper, good quality *Writing Royal* laid, watermark Strasbourg bend/LVG, size 24¼ × 19¼ in.

TYPE: As no. 24.

NOTE: Normally bound up with no. 24.

26 THE HOLY BIBLE, 2°, 1763

TITLE-PAGE: THE | [xylographic] Holy Bible, | CONTAINING THE | OLD TESTAMENT | AND | *THE NEW:* | Tranflated out of the | [xylographic] Original Tongues, | AND | With the former TRANSLATIONS | Diligently Compared and Revifed, | *By His MAJESTY's Special Command.* | [rule of 'lozenge and star' ornaments] | APPOINTED TO BE READ IN CHURCHES. | [rule of 'lozenge and star' ornaments] | *CAMBRIDGE,* | Printed by *JOHN BASKERVILLE,* Printer to the UNIVERSITY. | M DCC LXIII. | [plain rule] | *CUM PRIVILEGIO.*

FORMULA: Large Printing Royal 2°: A^2 χ1 B–13D² 13E1 *a–e² *f1 [signed with index figures from the third alphabet]. 573 leaves unnumbered.

CONTENTS: *A*1 title, *A*1ᵛ blank, *A*2–*A*2ᵛ The Epistle Dedicatory, *A*2ᵛ The Names and Order of the Books, χ1–χ1ᵛ Subscribers, B1–8S1ᵛ The Old Testament, 8S2–10O1 Apocrypha, 10O1ᵛ blank, 10O2 sub-title to the New Testament, 10O2ᵛ blank, 10P1–13E1 The New Testament, 13E1ᵛ blank, *a1–*e1 Index to the Holy Bible, *e1ᵛ–*e2ᵛ Scripture Measures, Weights, and Coins, *f1–*f1ᵛ Tables of Time, Offices and Kindred.

Note: In the Old and New Testaments there is, in addition to the Book title at the head of each page, an individual running title in italics over each column, i.e. four to an opening; in the Apocrypha, these running titles are replaced by the word '*Apocrypha.*'

VARIANTS: There are three versions of the Subscribers' list (χ1), the second containing more names than the first, and the third more than the second. The first ends with the name of Mr Winwood of Birmingham; the second with that of the Rev. David Yarrow of Hadley, Middlesex; and the third with that of the Hon. Charles York, Esq., Attorney General. The second of these versions is the least common.

ERRORS: Points in headlines (verso headlines should not have a point except for the Book of Psalms, and on versos on which a Book ends): superfluous points on the versos of 3I1, 6K1; points lacking on the versos of 2O1, 2Y1, 4T2, 8L2, 9N2, 9Y1, 12K2 and (in one example only) 7C2.

PAPER: Medium quality *Large Printing Royal* laid, no marks, size of sheet 26¼ × 20 in.

TYPE: Text, Dedication, *Great Primer*; headlines, *Double Pica*; footnotes and side-notes, *Small Pica*; Arguments, Subscribers, *English*; Index, Tables, *Pica*.

NOTES: Price to subscribers, four guineas in sheets (no. viii, above). The edition consisted of 1250 copies, of which 556 were remaindered in 1768 and bought by the London bookseller R. Baldwin at 36*s*. each (*Birmingham Gazette*, 1 January 1770). Baldwin was offering copies at three guineas in sheets in 1771 (*ibid.* 14 October 1771). See no. viii, above.

27 [ROBERT DODSLEY], SELECT FABLES, [SECOND EDITION], 8°, 1764

TITLE-PAGE: SELECT FABLES | OF | ESOP | AND | OTHER FABULISTS. | IN THREE BOOKS. | *—Is not the earth* | *With various living* creatures, *and the air* | *Replenifhed, and all thefe at thy command* | *To come and play before thee? Knoweft thou not* | *Their language and their ways? They alfo know,* | *And reafon not contemptibly: with thefe* | *Find paftime.* Paradife Loft, B. 8 l. 370. | [copperplate vignette, unsigned] | *BIRMINGHAM,* | Printed by JOHN BASKERVLLE [*sic*], for | R. and J. DODSLEY in Pall-mall. 1764.

FORMULA: Post 8°: $a^8(\pm a8)$ b–e⁸ B–O⁸ P⁴ [G3 unsigned]. Pp. [2] i–lxxviii 1–186 *187–216*.

CONTENTS: a1 title, a1ᵛ blank, i–iv Preface, v sub-title to the Life, vi blank, vii–liii The Life of Esop, liv blank, lv sub-title to the Essay, lvi blank, lvii–lxxvii An Essay on Fable, lxxviii blank, 1–186 Fables, Ancient, Modern and Original (pp. 2, 56, 58, 118 and 120 blank), *187–214* Index, *215–16* blank.

CANCEL: *Cancellandum* a8 not seen.

ERRORS: Points lacking in the headlines of pp. xxxiii, xlii, 43, 81, 177.

PLATES: The copperplates on the title-page and on pp. 3, 55, 59, 117, 121 and 186 are closely similar to those on the equivalent text pages of the edition of 1761 (see no. 14 above), but have all been recut. The fifteen inserted plates appear (when found) to have been printed from the copperplates used in 1761, now more worn. The frontispiece is recut.

PAPER: A light *Post* laid, now badly foxed, watermark a post-horn over the words SUPER FINE/AMSTERDAM; size of sheet at least 18¾ × 14¾ in.

TYPE: Text, *Long Primer* leaded; Life, *Small Pica* leaded; Preface, *English*.

NOTE: See Notes to no. 14 above.

28 DAVID JENNINGS, MEDALS, 8°, 1764

TITLE-PAGE: AN | INTRODUCTION | TO THE | KNOWLEDGE | OF | MEDALS. | [plain rule] | By the late Rev. *DAVID JENNINGS*, D.D. | [plain rule] | *LONDON:* | Printed by *JOHN BASKERVILLE;* | And Sold | By J. PAYNE, at the Feathers in Pater-nofter-Row; | and S. GARDNER, in Grace-church-Street. | M DCC LXIV.

VARIANT: The title-page is also found in another state, printed from the same type as that transcribed above down to 'Printed by *JOHN BASKERVILLE;*', but continuing:

| For | T. FIELD, in Cheapſide; and J. PAYNE, in Pater-|noſter-Row. M DCC LXIV.

The title-page does not appear as a cancel by itself, but it is of course possible that both leaves of section A were cancelled in some copies, the same settings of type being used for A2.

FORMULA: Post 8° in fours: A^2 B–H^4 I^2. Pp. [4] 1–60.

CONTENTS: A1 title, A1^v blank, A2 Advertisement, A2^v The Contents, 1–59 Of Medals, 60 advertisement for a collection of Jennings's lectures, and Errata.

CANCELS: See 'VARIANT', above.

PAPER: Medium quality *Post* laid; watermark a post-horn over LVG over a bell/IV; size of sheet 18½ × 15 in.

TYPE: Text, *Small Pica* leaded. There are also words in Greek and Hebrew, both without accents, cast on Baskerville's *Pica* body; they appear to be Caslon's *English* Greek and *English* Hebrew.

NOTE: Published by April 1764, price 2*s.* (*The Monthly Review*, vol. xxx, p. 329).

29 JOSEPH DALBY, THE VIRTUES OF CINNABAR AND MUSK, 4°, 1764 ('1762')

TITLE-PAGE: THE VIRTUES | OF | CINNABAR AND MUSK, | Againſt the BITE of a | MAD DOG, | ILLUSTRATED, | In a Letter to Sir *GEORGE COBB*, Baronet: | In which are recited upwards of a hundred Caſes, wherein this | Medicine hath happily ſucceeded: (whereof two were after the | *Hydro phobia* appeared;) together with ſome few Inſtances where-|in it hath not ſucceeded; owing entirely to its not being pro-|perly given, as is proved to Demonſtration: with proper Direc-|tions whereby to avoid the like Diſappoint ment for the Future. | WITH A WORD OR TWO | Concerning Dr. *HENRY BRACKEN*'s newly diſcovered *Speci-*|*fick*, of near eighteen hundred Years ſtanding; being a ſufficient | Refutation of the flimſy Arguments advanced by this celebrated | Writer, in a learned Rant on the Virtues of *Gooſe-greaſe*. | [rule of 'lozenge and star' ornaments] | By *JOSEPH DALBY*, Surgeon. | *Cauſa latet, vis eſt notiſſima.* | [rule of 'lozenge and star' ornaments] | *BIRMINGHAM;* | Printed by JOHN BASKERVILLE, for the Author: | and Sold by Z. STUART, in Pater-Noſter-Row, London; | Meſſ. FLETCHER, PARKER, and PRINCE, in Oxford. | M DCC LXIV.

Note: The title-page is also found in an earlier state, with line 7 set in *English* instead of *Great Primer* and ending with a full point instead of a colon, and with the last line reading:

M DCC LXII.

Both states are printed from the same setting of type (with these exceptions), and neither is found as a cancel. It is probable (*a*) that the changes were made during the run; and (*b*) that the page was corrected from the '1762' state to the '1764' state, rather than vice versa, since the book was reviewed as a new work in *The Monthly Review* for December 1764 (vol. XXXI, p. 472).

FORMULA: Printing Demy 4°: a⁴ B⁴(−B1) C–H⁴ [B1, although allowed for in the pagination, has been missing in every copy seen, including one that was uncut and unopened]. Pp. [8] 3–56.

CONTENTS: a1 title, a1ᵛ Advertisement, a2–a4ᵛ Subscribers, 3–40 A Letter to Sir George Cobb, Baronet, 41–55 Supplement, 56 To the Publick.

ERRORS: Seventeen misprints are often corrected with pen and ink in a contemporary hand. Most of the copies seen with these corrections appear to have been annotated by the same person, who has taken some care to imitate the proper sorts of letters for each correction. They are as follows:

P.	l.			
P. 4	l. 28	BOERHAVE	altered to	BOERHAAVE
5	26	[do.]		[do.]
6	16–17	be ſome by		by ſome be [sometimes]
12	35	*imminenti,*		*imminentis,*
12	36	Phrenetidæ		Phrenetide
13	39	natanti		natandi
35	17	abſtruce		abſtruſe
36	20	Critick's		Critick,
37	21	eſcharotick Quality		[erased]
37	41	infinite		infinitely
43	28	*Parvibbibuli*		*Parvibibuli*
44	11	CAPSON		COPSON
46	18	*Pernicem*		*Perniciem*
47	33	Tention		Tenſion
48	32	enſued, he		enſued. He
48	33	give		given
52	2	looked		look

PAPER: Medium quality *Printing Demy* laid; marks fleur-de-lys/IV; size of sheet 21¼ × 17¼ in.

TYPE: Text, *English*; footnotes, *Long Primer*; advertisement, *Great Primer*; pp. 13, 42, 52, etc., Baskerville's *Great Primer* Greek on his *English* body.

NOTE: Published by December 1764, price 2*s*. 6*d*. (*The Monthly Review*, vol. XXXI, p. 472).

30 ROBERT BARCLAY, APOLOGY, EIGHTH EDITION, 4°, 1765

TITLE-PAGE: AN | APOLOGY | FOR THE | True Chriſtian Divinity, | BEING AN | EXPLANATION and VINDICATION | OF THE | PRIN CIPLES and DOCTRINES | Of the PEOPLE called | *QUAKERS.* | Written in LATIN and ENGLISH | By *ROBERT BARCLAY,* | And ſince tranſlated into HIGH DUTCH, LOW DUTCH, FRENCH, | and SPANISH, for the Information of Strangers. | The EIGHTH EDITION in *ENGLISH.* | *BIRMINGHAM;* | Printed by JOHN BASKERVILLE, and ſold by the Bookſellers of | LONDON and WESTMINSTER. | M DCC LXV.

FORMULA: [? Printing Royal] 4°: a–c⁴ χ1 A–3T⁴ [χ1 (Errata) frequently missing]. Pp. [1–11] i–xiii [2] 1–504 *505–20*.

CONTENTS: a1 title, a1ᵛ blank, a2–b2 To the King, b2ᵛ R.B. Unto the Friendly Reader, b3–c4ᵛ Theses Theologicæ, χ1 Errata, χ1ᵛ blank, 1–501 Propositions I–XV, 502–4 The Conclusion, 505–6 A Table of the Authors, 507–20 A Table of the Chief Things.

CANCELS: In a few copies (so few that no statement of cancellation is included in the formula) the following leaves were cancelled: A3, B1, B3, C4, D3, O4, P2, Q1, Q3, 2D2, 2D4, 2E2, 2F3, 2R4, 2S2, 3E4, 3H3, 3H4, 3O1, 3O4, 3P1, 3P4, 3Q1 and 3R1; 3M4 may also have been cancelled in some copies, but I have not come across it. The *cancellantia* correct those mistakes referred to in a note at the foot of χ1, the Errata leaf: '*N.B.* Thoſe marked with *Aſteriſks*, are corrected in ſome Copies.'

Two separate versions of the Errata leaf, χ1, have been found. Textually they are identical. One was probably printed by Baskerville, being in his type, although on a wove paper that he did not commonly use around 1765. The other, set partly in Caslon, has the imprint: 'Phillips & Fardon, Printers, | George Yard, Lombard Street, London.', which suggests that it may have been printed much later;† this imprint is set very low on the page and would normally be trimmed away in a bound copy. In one copy (Fitzwilliam Museum, Cambridge) both versions of the Errata leaf are present together.

PAPER: Two lots of laid:

(*a*) A–R: medium quality, marks Strasbourg bend over star/LVG.

(*b*) S–3T, a–c: slightly poorer quality, marks Strasbourg bend/IV.

No uncut copy seen, but size of sheet at least $23\frac{1}{2}\times 19$ in.; probably *Printing Royal*. Both versions of the Errata leaf are on unwatermarked wove papers of good quality.

TYPE: Text, *English* leaded; Dedication, *Great Primer*; indexes, *Pica*; shoulder notes, *Long Primer*; p. 3, etc., Baskerville's *Great Primer* Greek on his *English* body.

NOTE: First edition: 8°, [? Aberdeen] 1678.

31 A VOCABULARY, 18°, 1765

TITLE-PAGE: A | VOCABULARY, | OR | Pocket Dictionary. | TO WHICH IS PREFIXED, | A COMPENDIOUS | GRAMMAR | OF THE | *ENGLISH* LANGUAGE. | *BIRMINGHAM;* | Printed by JOHN BASKERVILLE, and ſold | by Meſſieurs DOD, RIVINGTON, LONGMAN, | RICHARDSON, HAWES and Co. CROWDER, | ROBSON, and STUART, LONDON, 1765.

FORMULA: Writing Royal 18° in sixes: *A*² a–c⁶ d² B–N⁶ O² [a5 and b5 signed]. 96 leaves, unnumbered.

Note: Vertical chain lines and the position of the watermarks show the imposition of all but sigs. *A*, d and O to have been sheets of 18° with three signatures with cutting (see J. Johnson,

† James Phillips was apparently on his own at no. 2 George Yard both in 1775 and in 1785: H. R. Plomer, etc., *A Dictionary of the Printers and Booksellers...in England...1726 to 1775* (Oxford, 1932), p. 198, where he appears as a bookseller; and John Pendred, *Directory of the Book Trade* (ed. Graham Pollard, London, 1955), p. 3, where he is listed as a letterpress printer. Fardon's name does not appear in either list.

Typographia (London, 1824), vol. II, pp. *26–7). Sigs. *A*, d and O, which are printed on a different sort of paper and show horizontal chain lines, together make a half sheet of Writing Demy 12°, which is probably how they were printed.

CONTENTS: *A*1 title, *A*1ᵛ blank, *A*2–*A*2ᵛ The Preface, a1–b6ᵛ A General View of English Grammar, c1–d2 An Account of the most usual Mistakes (headline: Supplement), d2ᵛ blank, B1–O2ᵛ A Vocabulary.

PAPER: Two lots:
(*a*) a–c, B–N: medium quality *Writing Royal* laid, marks Strasbourg bend over star/LVG, size of sheet 23½ × 19½ in.
(*b*) *A*, d, O: medium quality *Writing Demy* laid, no marks, size of sheet 19¾ × 15½ in.

TYPE: Text, *Long Primer*; Preface, *Pica*; a1ʳ, 'arabesque' ornaments.

NOTE: Published, price 1*s*. unbound (Bennett, vol. II, p. 9), on about 21 April 1766 (*Birmingham Gazette*).

32 ROBERT ANDREWS, VIRGIL ENGLISHED, 8°, 1766

TITLE-PAGE: THE | WORKS | OF | VIRGIL, | ENGLISHED | By ROBERT ANDREWS. | [rule of 'lozenge and star' ornaments over plain rule] | *BIR MINGHAM;* | Printed by JOHN BASKERVILLE for the Author. | M DCC LXVI.

FORMULA: Printing Royal 8°: π1 2π^2 a^8 A^8(−A1) B–$2K^8$ $2L^4$ (with cancels at A2, A3, A5, A7, B1.8, B3.6, C3, D1, D2, D5, E8, H8, Y7, 2C8, 2D1) [X4 unsigned]. Pp. [6] (1)–(16) 3–536.
Note: A1 may originally have been intended to be part of the book, since it is allowed for in the main series of the pagination; possibly it was a sub-title that was cancelled but not replaced.

CONTENTS: π1 title, π1ᵛ blank, 2π1–2π2ᵛ Dedication, (1)–(16) The Author's Preface (no headline), 3–37 Pastorals, 38–126 I–IV Georgics, 127–528 I–XII Æneid, 529–36 Arguments and Notes (Errata at the foot of p. 536).

CANCELS: The pages in which major alterations are found in the *cancellantia* are 3, 4, 5, 6, 9, 13, 14, 17, 21, 22, 27, 28, 31, 32, 37, 38, 49, 51, 52, 57, 58, 79, 80, 127, 349, 350, 416, 417, 418. Cancellation appears to have been carried out at the author's request in order that he might correct his translation; in the early sections correction included the rewriting of whole lines and even paragraphs.
The copy at the Fitzwilliam Museum, Cambridge, is uncancelled; *cancellanda* are slashed with shears.

ERRORS: Misnumeration: '65' for 95, '255' for 259, '276' for 286, '270' for 290, '392' for 292, '204' for 294.

PAPER: Medium quality *Printing Royal* laid; watermark Strasbourg bend over LVG/IV; size of sheet 24 × 19½ in.

TYPE: Text, *English* leaded; Notes, *Long Primer*; Dedication, *Double Pica* leaded; a1, A2, 'arabesque' ornaments.

NOTE: Published by May 1766, price 7*s*. 6*d*. (*The Monthly Review*, vol. XXXIV, p. 405.)

33 Robert Andrews, ODES, 4°, 1766

Title-page: ODES, | Dedicated to the Honourable | CHARLES YORKE, Efq; | By ROBERT ANDREWS, | Author of the | ENGLISH VIRGIL, | Dedicated to the Honourable | BOOTH GREY, Efq; | [rule of 'lozenge and star' ornaments over plain rule] | *BIRMINGHAM;* | Printed for the Author, by JOHN BASKERVILLE, and | Sold by Meffirs JOHNSON & Co. Bookfellers, in Pater-Nofter-|Row, London. | M DCC LXVI. | Price One Shilling and Six Pence.

Variant: Title-page from a different setting, reading as above, except:
(*a*) Lines 2 and 7 have 'Dedicated', not 'Dedicated'.
(*b*) Line 3 reads 'CHARLES YORKE, Att. Gen.' (Yorke was Attorney-General throughout 1766.)

Formula: Writing Demy or Crown 4°: $A^2(\pm A^2)$ χ^2 B–D⁴(±D3) E1. Pp. 1–34.

Contents: 1 title, 2 Advertisement, 3–4 Dedication, 5–34 Odes.

Cancels: *Cancellandum* D3 not seen. It is not clear which of the two sections *A* cancels the other.

Paper: Two lots:
(*a*) *A* (both states), E and *cancellans* D3: medium quality laid, countermark IV, main mark not seen.
(*b*) χ, B–D: medium quality laid, no marks.
No uncut copy seen, but size of sheet is at least $19\frac{1}{2} \times 14\frac{1}{4}$ in., so probably *Writing Demy* or *Crown*.

Type: Text, *English* leaded; Dedication, *Double Pica* leaded.

Notes: Published by November 1766, price 1*s*. 6*d*. (*The Monthly Review*, vol. xxxv, p. 407). On *A*1ᵛ is an advertisement for a projected edition of Andrews's translation of *Virgil* (no. 32 above, originally published by May 1766, at 7*s*. 6*d*.) together with these *Odes*, to be published in one octavo volume at '10s. ftich'd in Blue Paper and 12s. Bound'.

34 Virgil, BUCOLICA, GEORGICA ET AENEIS, 8°, 1766

Title-page: PUBLII VIRGILII | MARONIS | BUCOLICA, | GEORGICA, | ET | AENEIS. | [copperplate vignette, unsigned] | *BIRMINGHAMIÆ;* | Typis JOHANNIS BASKERVILLE. | M DCC LXVI.

Formula: Post 8°: *A*1 B–2B⁸ 2C² (with cancels at D5, E4, G2, G4, I3 and I8) [I4 unsigned]. Pp. [2] 1–388.

Contents: *A*1 title, *A*1ᵛ blank, 1–27 Bucolica. Ecl. i–x, 28 blank, 29–94 Georgicon Lib. i–iv, 95–388 Æneidos Lib. i–xii (verso headline P. Virgilii throughout).

Cancels: *Cancellanda* E4 and G4 not seen. The major changes in D5 and I8 were:
D5: *-andum*, p. 41 l. 423 'litore corvi.'; *-ans*, 'gutture corvi.'
-andum, p. 42 l. 461 'trahat,'; *-ans*, 'vehat,'
I8: *-andum*, p. 127 l. 340 'Iphitus', l. 341 'Chorœbus'; *-ans*, 'Epytus', 'Corœbus'

In a copy of no. 27 (Dodsley's *Select Fables*, 1764) belonging to Lord Rothschild,† the *cancellanda* of leaves G2 and I3 of the 1766 *Virgil* have been pasted down inside the boards, in both cases showing the rectos. The first two or three letters of each line on I3r were cut away before the leaf was pasted down. The following are the major visible differences:
G2: *-andum*, p. 83 l. 218 'pulcramque', l. 221 'Ætherios'; *-ans*, 'pulchramque', 'Æthereos'
I3: *-andum*, p. 117 l. 752 'equi:', l. 753 'prima, dic,'; *-ans*, 'equi;', 'prima dic,'

PLATE: Frontispiece facing *A*1: copperplate, signed S. Wale, C. Grignion.

PAPER: Three lots of *Post* laid:

(*a*) B–S: thin, foxed, no marks.

(*b*) T–2C: thin, slightly better quality than (*a*), foxed, marks a post-horn over the words SUPER FINE/AMSTERDAM, as used for Dodsley's *Fables*, 1764, no. 27 above.

(*c*) *A*1 and frontispiece: medium quality; with watermarks, but not enough seen for identification.

No uncut copy seen, but size of sheet is at least 19½ × 14¾ in. None of these papers has stood the passage of time well.

TYPE: Text, *Bourgeois* leaded.

NOTES: In some copies there is an extra leaf inserted after *A*1, reading:

[rule of 'diamond' ornaments] | RECENSUIT *J. LIVIE*, A.M. | [rule of 'diamond' ornaments]

Neither the 'diamond' ornaments nor *Brevier No. 2*, in which the second line is set, were used in any book printed by Baskerville himself, though both are shown in the *Specimen* of 1777 (no. xvi above).

Shenstone to Thomas Percy, 10 August 1762: 'Baskerville has begun to print a Virgil of ye *size* of the Spectator' (Williams, *Letters of Shenstone*, p. 632).

Probably published in April 1766 (*Birmingham Gazette*, 21 April 1766). Copies were despatched to Livie by Baskerville early in December 1766 (Straus and Dent, p. 102). 800 copies remained in 1775 (pp. xvii–xviii above).

35 THE HOLY BIBLE, 2°, 1769–72

TITLE-PAGE: THE | [xylographic] Holy Bible, | CONTAINING THE | OLD TESTAMENT | AND | THE NEW; | WITH THE | APOCRYPHA: | Tranflated out of the | [xylographic] Original Tongues, | WITH | ANNOTA TIONS. | [rule of 'lozenge and star' ornaments] | *BIRMINGHAM*; | Printed by JOHN BASKERVILLE. | M DCC LXIX.

Note: The sub-title to the New Testament is dated 1771.

VARIANT: The title-page is also found in another state, printed from the same type but with the last line altered to:

M DCCLXXII.

The book was issued in parts, starting in January 1769 (see NOTES, below), the earlier state of the title-page being issued in the first part; it was probably reprinted in 1772 for use when the book was sold complete.

The 1772 title-page is found with a resetting of *A*2 (the first page of the text, from Genesis i. 1).

† *The Rothschild Library* (Cambridge, privately printed, 1954), vol. I, p. 193 (no. 807).

FORMULA: [? Large Printing Demy] folio: A^2 ($A1 + \chi 1$) B–13I^2 13K1 [signed with index figures from the third alphabet on. Misprints 'N' for O (sometimes), 'M4' for 4M, 'E6' for 6E, 'D9' for 9D and '11G' for 13G. The book is also signed with roman numerals for part-issue on every other section; thus *A* is no. I (though it is unsigned), C no. II, E no. III and so on up to 13I, which is no. CXLIII]. 572 leaves, unnumbered.

CONTENTS: *A*1 title, *A*1^v blank, χ1 Contents, χ1^v blank, *A*2–9C1^v The Old Testament, 9C2–10Y1 Apocrypha, 10Y1^v blank, 10Y2 sub-title to The New Testament, 10Y2^v blank, 10Z1–13K1 The New Testament, 13K1^v Tables.

Note: The headlines are arranged in the same way as in the 1763 edition, except that there are dates instead of descriptive running titles on either side of the Book titles, and that the use of the word '*Apocrypha.*' as a running title in that section is spasmodic.

PRESS FIGURES: The press figures '1' or '2' are found on sheets 4I, 4L, 4M, 4N and 5N to 13I inclusive; most of these sheets have two figures. The following is a sample run from the middle of the book, showing all the press figures in sheets 11A to 12G; the space between each pair of sheets divides the run into parts as issued.

11A1^v 2, 2^v 1	11L1^v 1, 2^v 1	11X1^v 1, 2^v 1
11B2 1, 2^v 1	11M1^v 1, 2^v 1	11Y2 1, 2^v 1
11C1^v 1, 2^v 1	11N2 2, 2^v 1	11Z1^v 1, 2^v 1
11D2 2, 2^v 1	11O1^v 1, 2^v 1	12A2 1, 2^v 1
11E1^v 1, 2^v 1	11P1^v 1, 2^v 1	12B2 1, 2^v 1
11F1^v 1, 2^v 2	11Q1^v 1, 2^v 1	12C1^v 2, 2^v 1
11G1^v 1, 2^v 1	11R1^v 1, 2^v 1	12D2 2, 2^v 1
11H1 1, 1^v 1	11S1 1, 1^v 1	12E1^v 1, 2^v 2
11I1^v 1, 2^v 1	11T1^v 1, 2^v 1	12F2 1, 2^v 1
11K1 1, 1^v 1	11U1^v 1, 2^v 1	12G1^v 1, 2^v 2

The reprinting of the same figure twice on each of twelve consecutive sheets seems odd. This is the only one of Baskerville's books that has press figures.

PLATES: Frontispiece and nine other copperplates, facing *A*1, B1, H1^v, 2P1, 3U1^v, 4B1^v, 10Y2, 10Z1^v, 11F2^v and 11L2^v. Signed by the artists F. Hayman, C. Vanloo, J. Jouvenet and J. M. Moreau le jeune; and by the engravers Westwood, I. Taylor, Le Grand, J. Caldwell, and Hicks. Sometimes plates from Boden's *Bible* are found in addition.

PAPER: Most of the book is on a poor quality *Printing Demy* laid, watermarks fleur-de-lys/IV; but three other papers were used occasionally, all of poor quality, one with marks similar to those of the main paper and the other two without marks. No uncut copy seen, but size of sheet is at least 21¼ × 16½ in.

Baskerville himself claimed, in the controversy with Boden (see NOTES, below), that he was using a 'superfine Demy Writing Paper' costing 'Fifteen Shillings and sixpence per Ream in London'. This paper is certainly not a superfine *Writing Demy*, as is shown by the watermarks and the size, as well as by the quality, and if Baskerville paid fifteen and six a ream for it he was robbed.

TYPE: Text, *English*; notes, *Bourgeois*.

NOTES: The first number appeared on about 2 January 1769, price twopence-halfpenny (*Birmingham Gazette*, no. 1415). For full details of publication, and of the controversy with Boden, see Straus and Dent, Appendix II, where the relevant documents are quoted in full.

36 Thomas Tyndal, A SERMON, 8°, 1769

Title-page: [within a frame of nonpareil rule, 150 × 85 mm.] *The Confideration of our Latter End recommen-|ded, as the means of obtaining true Wifdom.* | [plain rule] | A | SERMON | PREACHED AT | *BROMSGROVE,* | On Occafion [*sic*] of the | DEATH | OF | Mr. *JOHN SPILSBURY;* | WHO | Died the 27th of January, 1769, in the 75th | Year of his Age. | [plain rule] | By THOMAS TYNDAL. | [plain rule] | *BIRMINGHAM:* | Printed by John Baskerville. | MDCCLXIX.

Formula: Printing Demy or Crown 8° in fours: π^2 A–E^4. Pp. [4] 1–40.

Contents: π1 title, $\pi 1^v$ blank, π2 Advertisement, $\pi 2^v$ blank, 1–39 Sermon on the Death of Mr. John Spilsbury, 40 blank.

Errors: Headlines on pp. 31 and 33 lack point.

Paper: Medium quality laid, watermark a fleur-de-lys; this mark appears on *every* half sheet in the two copies seen, so perhaps this is the paper with fleurs-de-lys for both main mark and countermark found in no. 37. No uncut copy seen, but size of sheet is at least 19¼ × 15¼ in.

Type: Text, *Pica*; 'Advertisement', *English.*

37 W. Jackson, THE BEAUTIES OF NATURE, 8°, 1769

Title-page: THE | BEAUTIES of NATURE, | DISPLAYED IN | A SENTI MENTAL RAMBLE | THROUGH | HER LUXURIANT FIELDS; | WITH | A RETROSPECTIVE VIEW of HER, | AND THAT GREAT | ALMIGHTY BEING WHO GAVE HER BIRTH. | TO WHICH IS ADDED, | A Choice COLLECTION of THOUGHTS: | CONCLUDED WITH | POEMS on Various OCCASIONS. | [plain rule] | By *W. JACKSON,* of *Lichfield Clofe.* | [plain rule] | [plain rule] | *Quam natura miranda, veritas amanda!* | [plain double rule] | BIRMINGHAM: | Printed by J. BASKERVILLE, for the Author, by whom it is Sold, | and *M. Morgan,* Bookfeller, in *Lichfield.* | MDCCLXIX.

Formula: Large Printing Demy 8°: A^8 χ1 B–T^8 [A2^v signed 'A3'; G4 unsigned]. Pp. i–xvi [2] 1–288.

Contents: i title, ii blank, iii–iv Preface, v–xvi Names of the Subscribers, $\chi 1$–$\chi 1^v$ The Index, 1–288 text (no headlines).

Errors: Misnumeration: 270 and 271 transposed.

Headlines: p. 24, brackets transposed; p. 110, first bracket turned; p. 172, high space to the left of the page number.

Paper: Brownish, poor quality *Large Printing Demy* laid, watermark fleur-de-lys/IV, size of sheet 21 × 17¼ in. Section R sometimes on a rather better quality paper, which apparently has fleurs-de-lys for both the main mark and the countermark.

TYPE: Text, *English*; footnotes, *Brevier No. 1*; Preface, *Great Primer*; Subscribers, *Pica*; Index, *Long Primer*; p. 15, etc., *Great Primer* Greek on Baskerville's *English* body; p. 1, 'arabesque' ornaments.

NOTES: Published on about 4 September 1769, price 5*s*. sewed (*Birmingham Gazette*, no. 1450). Reviewed in *The Monthly Review* for March 1770 (vol. XLII, p. 167).

38 ANON., LIFE OF WILKES, 8°, 1769

TITLE-PAGE: THE | LIFE | AND | POLITICAL WRITINGS | OF | JOHN WILKES, Efq; | FOUR TIMES ELECTED | KNIGHT OF THE SHIRE | FOR THE | COUNTY OF MIDDLESEX, | AND | ALDERMAN ELECT OF THE WARD | OF | FARRINGDON WITHOUT, LONDON. | [plain double rule] | Thrice happy He, who in this fated hour, | Provokes the mighty thunderbolts of Pow'r; | With juft difdain behold [*sic*] the venal tribe, | And fpurns alike a Briber and a Bribe! | Whate'er he feels, with opennefs can fpeak, | And blufhes plants e'en on a Statefman's cheek. | Him the white record of the faithful page | Shall hand down honour'd to the lateft age. | [plain double rule] | BIRMINGHAM: | Printed for J. SKETCHLEY and Co. | [plain rule] | M, DCC, LXIX.

FORMULA: [? Printing Demy] 8° in fours: A^4 B–$3T^4$ [$1 signed, but also the second leaf of C, F, I, L, N–T, X, Z, 2B, 2G and 2I–2K]. Pp. [8] 1–522 (=512, see ERRORS below).

CONTENTS: *A*1 title, *A*1^v blank, *A*2–*A*3^v Dedication, *A*4–*A*4^v Preface, 1–522 The Life, &c. Of John Wilkes, Esq., including 520–22 To the Public (no new headline), 522 Errata (in fact, only one erratum).

ERRORS: Misnumeration: main series runs 1–176 178–89 *190* 190–255 266–522 (=512). Misprints '566' for 266, '390' for 400; '4' of 486 turned.
Headlines: pp. 15 and 35: '*WIKLES*' for *WILKES*.
*A*2, l. 2: '*Refpecte*', lacking final '*d*'.

PAPER: Three lots of brownish, poor quality laid:
(*a*) *A*–N, 3I–3T: watermark fleur-de-lys/IV.
(*b*) O–Q: watermark fleur-de-lys in a shield crowned, countermark not seen, a mark usually associated with *Writing Demy* and *Writing Medium*; this paper is too large for *Writing Demy*, but could be a very poor quality *Writing Medium*.
(*c*) R–3H: no marks.
No uncut copy seen, but size of sheet is at least 19¾ × 16¼ in., so probably *Printing Demy*.

TYPE: Text, *Small Pica*; Dedication and Preface, *English*. P. 522, a crude woodcut vignette tailpiece of Britannia.

NOTE: Wilkes's *Writings* were to have followed in later volumes. Ascribed to Baskerville on the evidence of the type; but the press-work is so poor that it may be Martin's work.

This description is of the British Museum copy. The copy at Birmingham Reference Library shows some minor variations: the second leaves of sections U, Y, 2A and 2C–2F are signed; p. 266 is numbered '56'; p. 400 is correctly numbered; and the paper is arranged in a slightly different way. It may therefore represent a different impression.

39 HORACE, 4°, 1770

TITLE-PAGE: QUINTUS | HORATIUS | FLACCUS. | [Copperplate vignette signed '*le grand sculp*'] | *BIRMINGHAMIÆ:* | Typis JOHANNIS BASKER VILLE. | MDCCLXX.

Note: The title-page exists in two settings, which are equally common. They are very similar but they can be told apart by the 'D' in the last line which is damaged in one of them. Possibly the title-page was set up in duplicate and printed with both versions on the press together.

FORMULA: Writing Royal 4°: π1 2π1 A–2A⁴ (±2A1) 2B–2U⁴. Pp. [4] 1–344.

CONTENTS: π1 title, π1ᵛ blank, 2π1 sub-title to Carmina, 2π1ᵛ blank, 1–147 Carminum Libri I–IV (pp. 46 and 74 blank), 148 blank, 149 sub-title to Epodoi, 150 blank, 151–80 Epodon Liber, 181–4 Carmen Seculare, 185 sub-title to Sermones, 186 blank, 187–266 Sermonum Libri I–II (p. 226 blank), 267 sub-title to Epistolae, 268 blank, 269–326 Epistolarum Libri I–II, 327–44 Ars Poetica (verso headline Q. Horatii Flacci throughout).

CANCEL: 2A1 (sub-title to *Sermones*): four different *cancellantia* are found, none of them differing from the *cancellandum* or from each other except in the arrangement of the units of the two rules of 'lozenge and star' ornaments. The leaf may have been cancelled on account of irregularity in the alternation of the top line of flowers, or because of poor press-work. It is possible that, in order to save time, the *cancellans* was set up four times and printed simultaneously on one side of a whole sheet.

ERROR: Page 232 misnumbered '234'. Headlines: extra point on pp. 11, 39, 79, 97, 123 and 141.

PLATES: Frontispiece (signed Henriquez) facing π1, and four other plates signed by Gravelot, and by the engravers Godfroy, Voyer, Leveau and le Vasseur, facing A1, 2A2, 2L3 and 3S4. The frontispiece was found in all, but the other plates in only half, of the copies examined. Gravelot's original drawings for the four plates are now in the Pierpont Morgan Library in New York.

PAPER: Two lots of medium quality *Writing Royal* laid; watermarks Strasbourg bend/JW; size of sheet 24½ × 19 in. One of them, of poorer quality than the other, is used only for sections G–O.

TYPE: Text, *Great Primer* leaded.

40 JOSEPH LIEUTAUD, ESSAY TOWARDS PUBLISHING A SYNOPSIS, TRANSLATED BY T. TOMLINSON, 1770 [NOT SEEN]

NOTES: The following advertisement appeared in the *Birmingham Gazette* for 17 September 1770 (no. 1504):

> *This Day is publiſhed, Price Six-pence,* AN ESSAY towards publiſhing A SYNOPSIS of the GENERAL PRACTICE OF PHYSIC. Tranſlated from the Latin of *Joſeph Lieutaud,* Chief Phyſician to the Royal Family of France. By T. TOMLINSON. Printed by J. Baſkerville, and ſold by W. Nicholl, No 51, St. Paul's Church Yard, London, and the Printers hereof [i.e. S. Aris of Birmingham].

No copy of this book is known to have survived.

41 [JOHN FELLOWS], GRACE TRIUMPHANT, 8°, 1770

TITLE-PAGE: GRACE TRIUMPHANT. | A SACRED | POEM, | In Nine DIALOGUES, | Wherein the utmoft Power of | NATURE, REASON, VIRTUE, | AND THE | LIBERTY of the HUMAN WILL, | To adminifter COMFORT to the awakened SINNER, | are impartially weighed and confidered; | AND | The Whole fubmitted to the ferious and candid Pe-|rufal of the Reverend Dr. *Nowel* of *Oxford:* the Re-|verend Dr. *Adams* of *Shrewfbury:* and the Author of *Pietas Oxonienfis.* | By PHILANTHROPOS. | *For a fmall moment have I forfaken thee; but with great mercies will* | *I gather thee. In a little wrath I hid my face from thee for a moment;* | *but with everlafting kindnefs will I have mercy on thee, faith the Lord thy* | *Redeemer.* Ifaiah, liv. 7, 8. | [plain rule] | *BIRMINGHAM:* | PRINTED for the AUTHOR. | MDCCLXX.

FORMULA: Printing Demy 8° in fours: π1 A–Q⁴ R1 [A1 signed 'A2', A2 unsigned]. Pp. 1–10 1–122.

CONTENTS: π1 title, π1ᵛ blank, A1–A2ᵛ To the Rev. Mr. John Ryland (no headline), A3–A4 Preface (no headline), A4ᵛ blank, 1–122 Grace Triumphant. Dialogues the First (to) the Ninth (pp. 16, 50, 60 and 122 blank).

PAPER: Two lots of poor quality *Printing Demy* laid, now rather foxed:
(*a*) A–Q: watermark fleur-de-lys/IV.
(*b*) π, R: a similar paper, watermark fleur-de-lys, countermark not seen.
No uncut copy seen, but size of sheet is at least 21¼ × 16½ in.

TYPE: Text, *Small Pica* leaded; Dedication and Preface, *Pica.*

NOTES: Published by January 1771, price 2*s.* (*The Monthly Review*, vol. XLIV, p. 89). Assigned to Baskerville on the evidence of the type.

42 J. FREE [JOHN FREETH], THE POLITICAL SONGSTER, 8°, 1771

TITLE-PAGE: THE | POLITICAL SONGSTER; | ADDRESSED TO THE | SONS of FREEDOM, | AND | LOVERS of HUMOUR, | By *J. FREE.* | [plain rule] | *BIRMINGHAM:* | Printed for the AUTHOR, by J. BASKERVILLE, | and Sold by S. ARIS, and M. SWINNEY. | MDCCLXXI.

FORMULA: [? Printing Demy] 8° in fours: *A*² B–P⁴. Pp. 1–4 1–112.

CONTENTS: *A*1 title, *A*1ᵛ blank, *A*2–*A*2ᵛ To the Public, 1–112 The Political Songster.

ERRORS: P. 47 catchword 'Fo' for 'For'.
Headlines: p. 27 broken '*T*'; pp. 47, 57, 79 and 91 lack point.

PAPER: Medium quality laid, no marks; no uncut copy seen, but size of sheet is at least 20¼ × 16¼ in., so probably *Printing Demy.*

TYPE: Text, *Small Pica* leaded and solid: 'To the Public', *Pica*; p. 1, 'fleur-de-lys' and 'arabesque' ornaments.

NOTE: The Bodleian copy (280. i. 141) has an extra leaf, numbered 113–14, containing the song 'Beelzebub's Tour' bound in at the end; it was apparently printed by Baskerville.

43 LUCRETIUS, DE RERUM NATURA, 4°, 1772

TITLE-PAGE: TITI | LUCRETII CARI | DE | *RERUM NATURA* | LIBRI SEX. | [rule of 'lozenge and star' ornaments] | *BIRMINGHAMÆ:* [*sic*] | Typis JOHANNIS BASKERVILLE. | MDCCLXXII.

FORMULA: Writing Royal 4°: π1 A–2M⁴. Pp. [2] 1–280.

CONTENTS: π1 title, $\pi 1^v$ blank, 1–280 T. Lucretii Libri Primus–Sextus (p. 232 blank).

ERRORS: Headlines: pp. 13 and 29 lack point; p. 131 '*TERTIUS*' for *QUARTUS*. Two pairs of errors are each from the same settings of type: pp. 63 and 81, '*SCUNDUS*', pp. 65 and 85, '*LIBRR*'; since they are on H4/L1 and I1/L3, it is clear that they were moved haphazardly from page to page and not as part of a 'skeleton'.

PAPER: Three lots of good quality *Writing Royal* laid:
(*a*) A–F, N–S, 2A–2M and π: no marks.
(*b*) G–M: Strasbourg bend over LVG/IV.
(*c*) T–Z: as (*b*), but wider fleur-de-lys above the bend; occasionally foxed.
Size of sheet, 24½ × 19½ in.

TYPE: Text, *Great Primer* leaded; p. 172, *Great Primer* Greek.

NOTE: Published at a guinea; 800 copies remained in 1775 (pp. xvii–xviii above).

44 CATULLUS, TIBULLUS AND PROPERTIUS, OPERA, 4°, 1772

TITLE-PAGE: CATULLI, | TIBULLI, | ET | PROPERTII | OPERA. | [rule of 'lozenge and star' ornaments] | *BIRMINGHAMIAE:* | Typis JOH ANNIS BASKERVILLE. | MDCCLXXII.

FORMULA: Writing Royal 4°: π1 $A^4(\pm A2)$ B–$H^4(\pm H3)$ I–2X⁴ [misprint '2B' for B2]. Pp. [2] 1–200 221–372 (=352).

CONTENTS: π1 title, $\pi 1^v$ blank, 1–102 Catulli Liber, 103 sub-title to Tibullus, Liber I, 104 blank, 105–83 Tibulli Libri I–IV, 184 blank, 185 sub-title to Propertius, Liber I, 186 blank, 187–372 Propertii Libri I–IV (p. 334 blank).

CANCELS: A2: *-andum*, p. 4 l. 13 '&', l. 15 'amenus'; *-ans*, 'et', 'amemus'
H3: *-andum*, p. 61 l. 18 'Charybdis,'; *-ans*, 'Charybdis.'

ERRORS: Misnumeration: main series runs 1–200 221–372 (=352).
Headlines: p. 239, 'I.' for 'II.'; p. 311, 'III' for 'III.'; p. 338, 'VI.' for 'IV.'

PAPER: Good quality *Writing Royal* laid, no marks, size of sheet 24 × 19¼ in.

TYPE: Text, *Great Primer* leaded.

NOTE: Published at a guinea; 780 copies remained in 1775 (pp. xvii–xviii above).

45 CATULLUS, TIBULLUS AND PROPERTIUS, OPERA, 12°, 1772

TITLE-PAGE: CATULLI, | TIBULLI, | ET | PROPERTII | OPERA. | [rule of 'lozenge and star' ornaments] | *BIRMINGHAMIAE:* | Typis JOH ANNIS BASKERVILLE. | MDCCLXXII.

Note: Two settings of the title-page are found, textually identical; one of them has a wrong-fount (too large) 'T' in 'CATULLI'. They appear to be equally common.

FORMULA: Writing Medium 12° in sixes: π1 A^6($\pm$A2) B–Z^6 [G2, P2 and X3 unsigned]. Pp. [2] 1–276.

CONTENTS: π1 title, $\pi 1^v$ blank, 1–79 Catulli Liber, 80 blank, 81 sub-title to Tibullus, Liber I, 82 blank, 83–145 Tibulli Libri I–IV, 146 blank, 147 sub-title to Propertius, Liber I, 148 blank, 149–276 Propertii Libri I–IV.

CANCEL: A2: *-andum*, p. 4 l. 2 'amenus'; *-ans*, 'amemus'.

ERRORS: Misnumeration '109' for 209.
Headlines: pp. 31, 65, 111, 153 and (sometimes) 189, '*EIBER*' for *LIBER*. P. 7, no point; pp. 84 and 134, extra points (or high space on 134); p. 262, comma for point; p. 144, 'V' for IV.
Catchwords: p. 212 'Uua' for 'Una' (sometimes correct).

PAPER: Medium quality *Writing Medium* laid; main watermark and countermark are each single capital letters, one an 'H', the other a 'D'; size of sheet 21¾ × 17¼ in.

TYPE: Text, *Bourgeois.*

NOTE: 800 copies remained in 1775 (pp. xvii–xviii above).

46 TERENCE, COMŒDIÆ, 4°, 1772

TITLE-PAGE: PUBLII | TERENTII | AFRI | COMOEDIAE. | [rule of 'lozenge and star' ornaments] | *BIRMINGHAMIAE:* | Typis JOH ANNIS BASKERVILLE. | M DCC LXXII.

FORMULA: Writing Royal 4°: π1 A–$2Y^4$ $2Z^2$. Pp. [2] 1–364.

CONTENTS: π1 title, $\pi 1^v$ blank, 1–60 Andria, 61–126 Eunuchus, 127–90 Heautontimorumenos, 191–250 Adelphi, 251–312 Phormio, 313–64 Hecyra (verso headline P. Terentii throughout).

ERRORS: Misnumeration: '303' for 203, '283' for 299.

PAPER: Good quality *Writing Royal* laid, in two main lots:
(*a*) A–U: watermark Strasbourg bend over LVG, from at least four (differently) damaged moulds; no countermark.
(*b*) X–2Z, π: similar watermark, slightly different paper; no countermark.
Size of sheet: (*a*) 24¼ × 19¼ in.; (*b*) 24 × 19 in.

TYPE: Text, *Great Primer* leaded.

NOTES: Published at a guinea; 860 copies remained in 1775 (pp. xvii–xviii above). Wormholes in a copy of this book which belongs to Mr William P. Barlow Jr., of Piedmont, California, show that it was originally kept for some time in sheets, separately folded once across the longer dimension and then arranged in the proper order. (E.g. a wormhole which passes through leaves Y1 and Y2 misses Y3 and Y4, but reappears to pass through Z1 and Z2; and a different wormhole passes through Y3 and Y4, Z3 and Z4, 2A3 and 2A4 and so on.)

47 TERENCE, COMŒDIÆ, 12°, 1772

TITLE-PAGE: PUBLII | TERENTII | AFRI | COMOEDIÆ. | [rule of 'lozenge and star' ornaments] | *BIRMINGHAMIAE:* | Typis JOHAN NIS BASKERVILLE. | MDCCLXXII.

Note: The 'R' (and sometimes also the 'F') of 'AFRI' damaged.

FORMULA: Writing Medium 12° in sixes: π^2 A–G^6 (±G2) H–$2B^6$ $2C^4$ [O3 and P3 unsigned]. Pp. [4] 1–308.

Note: The watermarks and torn edges in an uncut copy belonging to Mr William P. Barlow Jr., of Piedmont, California, show that 2C was actually printed as a six-leaf section and that 2C3.4 were then removed to become π^2.

CONTENTS: π1–$\pi 1^v$ blank, π2 title, $\pi 2^v$ blank, 1–50 Andria, 51–104 Eunuchus, 105–57 Heauton-timorumenos, 158 blank, 159–208 Adelphi, 209–61 Phormio, 262 blank, 263–307 Hecyra, 308 blank (verso headline P. Terentii throughout).

CANCELS: G2: *-andum*, p. 75 l. 22 'ub i' (sometimes corrected); *-ans*, 'ubi'
-andum, p. 76 headline: extra point after '*TERENTII*'; *-ans*, no extra point
-andum, p. 76 l. 11 'lib et' (sometimes corrected); *-ans*, 'libet'

ERRORS: Misnumeration: '191' for 291.

Headlines: p. 127, '*HEAUTONTIMORUMEONS*' for *HEAUTONTIMORUMENOS*; p. 267, '*HECIRA*' for *HECYRA*; p. 293, lacks point.

Recurring errors in verso headlines, which should read '*P. TERENTII*':

(*a*) '*TERENTII*': pp. 26, 62, 112, 170, 224, 270; all from the same setting, except that on p. 26 (which also adds a point).

(*b*) '*P· TERENTII*': pp. 50, 98, 164, 206, 268; all from the same setting.

(*c*) '*P. TERENTII.*': pp. 28, 30, 32, 76 (*cancellandum*), 78, 80, 128, 130, 132, 166, 172, 190, 208; three settings, which occur first on pp. 28, 30 and 32, are repeated in the same order on pp. 76, 78 and 80, and are jumbled up in the other seven occurrences.

The positions of these recurring errors show that Baskerville did not leave these page headlines in the skeleton formes.

PAPER: Two lots of medium quality *Writing Medium* laid:

(*a*) A–G: no marks.

(*b*) H–2C, π: 'H' and 'D' marks, as in no. 45 above.

Size of sheet: (*a*) 22¼ × 17½ in.; (*b*) 21¾ × 17¼ in.

TYPE: Text, *Bourgeois*.

NOTE: A thousand copies remained in 1775 (pp. xvii–xviii above).

48 ARIOSTO, ORLANDO FURIOSO, 4 VOLUMES, 8° AND 4°, 1773 (1771)

INTRODUCTION: The Ariosto was issued, probably in 1773, in octavo and in quarto. Its title-pages were normally dated 1773, but copies of both the 4° and the 8° exist with variant title-pages dated 1771. It seems likely that the letterpress was printed in 1770, and the plates completed late in 1773 (see no. xv above, 'variants'). The octavo issue is usually found with only two cancels, although some copies (1773 only) have a further fifty-three cancels as well. The quarto issue of 1773 has all these cancels, plus eleven more, a total of sixty-six.

TITLE-PAGES: (*a*) OCTAVO

ORLANDO | FURIOSO | DI | LODOVICO | ARIOSTO. | [thick and thin rule, mitred] | *TOMO PRIMO* [*SECONDO*] [*TERZO*] [*QUARTO*]. | [thick and thin rule, mitred] | *BIRMINGHAM,* | Da' Torchj di G. BASKERVILLE: | Per P. MOLINI Librajo dell' Accademia | Reale, e G. MOLINI. | [thick and thin rule, mitred] | M.DCC.LXXIII.

Note: Each title is from a different setting.

(*b*) QUARTO

[From the same settings.]

VARIANTS: Copies of both issues are known with title-pages from different settings, dated 1771; only one copy of each issue in this state seen, neither of them having more cancels than the first two in vol. IV. The imprint of the 1771 titles read:

BIRMINGHAM, | Da' Torchj ['Trochj' in vol. II] di G. BASKERVILLE: | A ſpeſe di PIETRO, e GIOVANNI MOLINI. | [thick and thin rule, mitred] | M.DCC.LXXI.

FORMULAE: (*a*) OCTAVO

[? Printing Royal] 8°:

Vol. I: π1 2π1 3π1 a–g^4 χ1 *^{8} 2*^{4} 3*^{2} A–Y^8 Z^4 2χ^2. [Asterisk sections signed as follows: *, ** [=*2], *** [=*3], **** [=*4], –, –, –, –; 2*, 2** [=2*2], –, –; *3 [=3*], –.] [3*2 errata]. Pp. [6] i–lviii *lix–lxxxvi* 1–362.

Vol. II: π1 A–2E^8 2F^2. Pp. [2] 1–452. Vol. III: π1 A–2E^8. Pp. [2] 1–448.

Vol. IV: π1 A^8(±A8) B–D^8 (±D2) E–2D^8 2F–2G^4. Pp. [2] 1–448.

Note: The three sections signed with asterisks, here placed after χ1 in vol. I, are sometimes found elsewhere (e.g. at the end of vol. IV).

For the fifty-three cancels found only occasionally in this issue, see CANCELS, below.

(*b*) QUARTO

Writing Royal 4°:

Vol. I: π1 2π^2 a–g^4 χ1 A–2Y^4 2Z1. Pp. [6] i–lviii 1–362.

Vol. II: π1 A–3K^4 3L1. Pp. [2] 1–450. Vol. III: π1 A–3K^4(–3K4). Pp. [2] 1–446.

Vol. IV: π1 A–3H^4 ^{2}2F–^{2}2G^4(–^{2}2G4) *^{4} 3*^{4} 4*^{4} 5*1 (or 5*^{2} if without cancels) [asterisk sections signed as follows: *, ** [=*2], –, –; ***, **** [=3*2], –, –; ****, –, –, –; *****, –]. [5*2 errata]. Pp. [2] 1–446 [1–26 (or 28)].

Note: As in the octavo, the asterisk sections may be found elsewhere in the book.

For the sixty-six cancels usually found in this issue, see CANCELS, below.

CONTENTS: (*a*) OCTAVO:

Vol. I: π1 title, π1^v blank, 2π1–2π1^v Sacra Reale Maestra, 3π1 L'Editore a' Lettori, 3π1^v blank, i–lii Vita di Lodovico Ariosto, liii–lvii Avvertimenti di Geronimo Ruscelli, lviii Leonis X Epistola (without headlines up to p. lviii), lix–lxxxiv Associati, lxxxv–lxxxvi Errata, 1–362 Orlando Furioso Canti Primo–Duodecimo.

Vol. II: π1 title, π1^v blank, 1–450 Orlando Furioso Canti Terzodecimo–Ventesimoterzo, *451–2* blank.

Vol. III: π1 title, π1^v blank, 1–446 Orlando Furioso Canti Ventesimoquarto–Trentesimoquinto, *447–8* blank.

Vol. IV: π1 title, π1^v blank, 1–426 Orlando Furioso Canti Trentesimosesto–Quarantesimosesto, 427–31 Stanze di Luigi Gonzaga, 432 blank, 433–46 Tavola (no headline), *447–8* blank.

(*b*) QUARTO:

Vol. I: π1 title, $\pi 1^v$ blank, $2\pi 1$–$2\pi 1^v$ Sacra Reale Maestra, $2\pi 2$ L'Editore a' Lettori, $2\pi 2^v$ blank, i–lviii, 1–362 as the octavo.

Vol. II: As the octavo, minus the final blank.

Vol. III: As the octavo, minus the final blank.

Vol. IV: As the octavo up to p. 446, then: *–5*1^v Associati, 5*1^v Errata (assuming that we are dealing with a copy that has cancels, but lacks the main Errata leaf, which, when it is present, is 5*2).

CANCELS: (*a*) OCTAVO

The octavo issue normally has only A8 and D2 in vol. IV cancelled, the errata later corrected by cancellation being listed on pp. *lxxxv–vi* (3*2) of vol. I; some copies, however, have up to fifty-three further cancels. All fifty-five are listed in the Table below.

(*b*) QUARTO

The quarto issue has as a rule all the cancels found in this edition, a total of sixty-six. Where they correspond, they are exactly the same as the octavo cancels, only the signature being changed where necessary. They are in two main series, one series being printed on a different lot of paper from the other and having an asterisk in the signature line.†

The following table lists only the chief differences between *cancellanda* and *cancellantia*. Columns 1 and 2 give the signature references in the octavo and quarto respectively, with asterisks where they occur; column 3 gives the page reference; columns 4 and 5, the numbers of the stanza and of the line within the stanza; and columns 6 and 7 the *cancellandum* and *cancellans* readings.

VOLUME I

8° sig.	4° sig.	Page	Stanza	Line	*Cancellandum*	*Cancellans*
—	B1	9	xxiii	3	differenzia	differenza
B1	C1	17	xlvii	8	porrian	potrian
—	C3	22	lxiii	8	il ſuo	al ſuo
—	E1*	33	xiii	7	gagliarda	gagliardo
D1	G1	50	lxii	5	meſſaggero	meſſagiero
E5	K1	74	lvi	6	meteria	materia
E6	K2	75	lix	4	ſtripe	ſtirpe
F3	L3	86	viii	8	contra queſto	contro a queſto
—	N1	97	xlii	6	Valle ove	Valle, ove [*see* notes below]
H6	Q2	124	xlv	5	De ſe	Da ſe
L4	X4	168	lxxxi	3	ragionando riuſciro	ragionando ne veniro
M2	Z2	180	xxxii	7	inveſcati	ineſcati
M3	Z3	182	xxxix	1	Qella	Quella
M7	2A3	189	lix	7	colla ed	collo, ed
—	2B3	198	ii	4	ed arte	e da arte [*see* notes below]
N4	2B4	200	viii	1	Qual	Quel
Q4*	2H4*	248	lviii	7	chè de	chè di
R8*	2L4*	271	xxx	1	perſuppongo	preſuppongo
—	2M2*	275	xlii	2	al Donna	la Donna [*see* notes below]
S4	2M4	279	liv	2	inante!	innante!
S6	2N2	283	lxvii	7	Faccia	Facea
—	2O2*	291	xci	5	i lCiel	il ciel

† Some of the asterisks themselves have disappeared from the 'asterisk series' in the quarto, but the paper on which they are printed confirms their identity; see notes below.

VOLUME II

8° sig.	4° sig.	Page	Stanza	Line	*Cancellandum*	*Cancellans*
A2*	A2*	3	vi	1	Moi	Mio
D5*	H1*	58	lxxxii	2	Dopo in	Dopo il
D6	H2*	59	lxxxiv	3	A'vea	Avea
E2*	I2*	68	cxi	4	prezzi	pezzi
E8	K4*	80	ix	2	Lonbardi	Lombardi
—	Q2*	123	xxxi	8	Nel le	Nelle
H8*	Q4*	127	xli	4	che non	che con
I7*	S3*	141	lxxxv	6	Qeſto	Queſto
L3	X3*	165	lix	1	èvea	avea
M5	2A1*	185	cxix	6	altre	alte
N3*	2B3*	198	xxi	2	Che con	Che non
P8*	2G4*	240	cxlviii	8	liſciò	laſciò
R1*	2K1*	257	—	8	*luogo*	*lungo*
—	2Y2*	355	xxxi	7	compiaci	compiacci

VOLUME III

8° sig.	4° sig.	Page	Stanza	Line	*Cancellandum*	*Cancellans*
B1	C1	18	lii	6	Pien da	Pien di
B2	C2	19	liii	2	ame	arme
B5	D1	26	lxxv	3	Quantuque	Quantunque
—	D4	31	xc	4	Vade	Vada
C2*	E2*	36	cvi	6	Madricardo	Mandricardo
—	F3	45	xi	3	pinge	ſpinge
D4*	G4*	55	xlii	8	Bradamente	Bradamante
E3	I3*	70	lxxxvi	7	ſuo	ſua
G4	N4*	104	lxxxvii	2	povar	provar
G5*	O1*	106	xciii	4	ſocccorſo	ſoccorſo
N2	2B2*	195	lxxiii	1	Povate	Provate
N5*	2C1*	201	xci	8	campgana	campagna
O2	2D2*	212	xv	7	nodo	modo
P1	2F1	226	lvi	2	arion	airon
Q3	2H3	246	xxxviii	4	Frenciofa	Franciofa
R7	2L3	270	viii	3	ſudo	ſcudo
S5	2N1	281	xliii	1	ſtano	ſtrano
X3*	2S3*	326	lxiv	6	Ohe	Che
Z1*	2Y1*	353	xxix	4	ventò	vantò
Z5*	2Z1*	361	lv	1	e la	e le
2A8*	3B4*	383	cxix	6	orrbil	orribil

VOLUME IV

8° sig.	4° sig.	Page	Stanza	Line	*Cancellandum*	*Cancellans*
A8*	B4*	—	—	—	[not seen]	—
D2*	G2*	—	—	—	[not seen]	(4° signed '*D2')
H2*	P2*	115	xxx	2	ſtetto	ſtretto
M2*	Z2*	180	l	3	appeſſo	appreſſo
N6*	2C2*	203	xii	1	vittorria	vittoria
N8*	2C4*	208	xxvii	1	nella	nelle
S8*	2N4*	287	clvii	4	Barndimarte	Brandimarte
Y2*	2U2*	340	iii	2	Albano	Albino
3*1	5*1	verso	—	—	(without list of errata)	(with list of four errata)

[The last cancel may be found in vol. I.]

Notes on the table: An asterisk in column 1 or 2 indicates that the *cancellans* of the leaf in question may have an asterisk in the signature line. The following *cancellantia* of the 4° are also found without asterisks: vol. I, E1, 2M2, 2O2; vol. II, H2, K4, Q2, X3, 2A1, 2Y2; vol. III, I3, 2B2, 2D2.

4°, vol. I, N1 and 2M2: these leaves are not mentioned in the list of errata.

4°, vol. I, 2B3: the list of errata says that the correction should be 'e ad arte'.

ERRORS: Misnumeration: vol. III, p. 87 turned '8', '296' for 269; vol. IV, '229' for 329.

PLATES: Copperplate frontispiece (portrait of Ariosto), and forty-six other plates. They are signed by the artists G. Cipriani, J. M. Moreau le jeune, C. Eisen, C. N. Cochin, C. Monnet, J. B. Gruize; and by the engravers F. Bartolozzi, N. de Launay, de Longueil, E. de Ghendt, B. L. Prevost, B. L. Henriquez, Massard, J. B. Simonet, N. Ponce, J. G. Duclos, P. A. Martini, P. S. Choffard and Helman. Each plate illustrates a passage from one of the forty-six *canti* of the poem, and is placed facing the opening of the canto to which it belongs. Many of them are dated 1771, 1772, 1773 or 1774.

A copy of the octavo belonging to Mr A. N. L. Munby, bound in two volumes in about 1790, contains the usual frontispiece, but only four plates (nos. 2, 35, 36 and a new one), which are printed on silk and mounted on inset leaves.

PAPER: (*a*) OCTAVO

Most of the book is on (*a*) a medium quality laid, no marks; but there are three other papers:

(*b*) Vol. I, π–g, 3*; vol. II, π; vol. III, π; vol. IV, π, 2F–2G: similar to (*a*), wider chain lines.

(*c*) Vol. I, *–2*: medium quality, marks Strasbourg bend over LVG/IV.

(*d*) Vol. IV, *cancellantia* A8 and D2: similar to (*a*) and (*b*), but not identical with either.

Unstarred *cancellantia* are on paper (*a*), starred *cancellantia* on paper (*b*).

No uncut copy seen, but size of sheet is at least 24 × 18¾ in.; this appears to be *Printing*, not *Writing*, *Royal*.

(*b*) QUARTO

Five lots of good quality *Writing Royal* laid:

(*a*) Vol. I, a–g; vol. IV, ²2F–²2G: no marks.

(*b*) Vol. I, A–2Z; vol. II, A–K, 2K–2L, 2U–3B, 3D; vol. III, E–K, N–P, 2H–3D, 3F; vol. IV, 2H: marks Strasbourg bend over LVG/[?].

(*c*) Vol. II, L–2I, 2M–2R, 2T, 3C, 3E–3K; vol. III, A–D, L–M, Q–2G, 3E, 3G–3K; vol. IV, A–2G: marks Strasbourg bend over GR/[?].

(*d*) Vol. IV, 2I–3H: similar to paper (*b*).

(*e*) Vol. IV, *–5*: as paper (*c*) of the octavo.

Cancellantia unstarred in the octavo, and new *cancellantia*, are on paper (*d*); *cancellantia* starred in the octavo are on paper (*e*).

No uncut copy seen, but size of sheet is at least 23¼ × 18¼ in.

(*c*) PLATES

Most of the plates are on a French 'grape' plate paper.

TYPE: Text, *English*; Subscribers, Life, *Pica* (footnotes, *Long Primer*); Index, *Bourgeois*.

Catchwords on the last page of each section only.

NOTES: The two editions of the *Proposals* suggest that the printing of the book was completed by about the end of 1770 and that it was issued, complete with plates, late in 1773 (see nos. xiv and xv, above). The price to subscribers was probably 4 guineas with the plates.

49 LORD SHAFTESBURY, CHARACTERISTICKS, 3 VOLUMES, 8°, 1773

TITLE-PAGES: [General] Characteriſticks | OF | *Men, Manners, Opinions, Times.* | In THREE VOLUMES. | By the Right Honourable | *ANTHONY*, Earl of SHAFTESBURY. | The FIFTH EDITION. | [copperplate emblem, signed Gribelin] | *BIRMINGHAM:* | Printed by JOHN BASKERVILLE. | M.DCC.LXXIII.

[Vol. I] Characteriſticks. | VOLUME I. | A Letter concerning ENTHUSIASM. | *Senſus Communis;* an Eſſay on the Freedom of | WIT and HUMOUR. | *Soliloquy*, or Advice to an AUTHOR. | [copperplate vignette, signed Gribelin] | Printed in the Year M.DCC.XXVII [*sic*] | A4

[Vol. II] Characteriſticks. | VOLUME II. | An Inquiry concerning VIRTUE and MERIT. | The MORALISTS; a Philoſophical Rhapſody. | [copperplate vignette, signed Gribelin] | Printed in the Year M.DCC.LXXIII.

[Vol. III] Characteriſticks. | VOLUME III. | MISCELLANEOUS REFLECTIONS on the pre-|ceding Treatiſes, and other Critical Subjects. | A Notion of the Tablature, or Judgment of | HERCULES. | [copperplate vignette, signed Gribelin] | Printed in the Year M.DCC.LXXIII.

Note: Some of the type used for the titles of vols. II and III is also used for the general title.

FORMULAE: Printing Royal 8°:

Vol. I: A^8(−A1) B–C^8(±C3) D–E^8(±E1, E2+'[E]'^{2}) F–K^8(K6+χ^2) L–P^8 Q^4 '[Q]'^{4} R–Z^8. Pp. [4] i–iv 1–366.

Note: Section A was probably printed as one odd leaf plus three pairs of leaves (general title; volume title—preface; contents—sub-title; text—text; or it is possible that the sub-title was the odd leaf and that the general title was paired with the contents); but the signatures make it clear how the section was intended to be put together.

Vol. II: π^2 A^2 B–I^8(±I1) K–M^8(M4+'[M]'^{2}) N–Q^8(±Q8) R–2E^8 [A1 signed 'A3']. Pp. 1–178 181–446 (=444).

Vol. III: π^2 A^2 B–D^8($\pm$D4) E–Z^8(Z2+χ^2) 2A–2B^8 *2B^2 *B^8 2C–2H^4 [χ2 signed 'Z3']. Pp. [4] 1–410 *411–60*.

Note: *2B^2 is an outset folded round *B^8; *B1 is signed '*B2',' *B2 is signed '*B3'.

CONTENTS:

Vol. I: A2 general title, A2^v blank, A3 general contents, A3^v blank, A4 title to volume I, A4^v blank, A5–A5^v Preface, A6 sub-title to Treatise I, A6^v blank (A7–A8^v are the first two leaves of text), 3–55 A Letter Concerning Enthusiasm, 56 blank, 57 sub-title to Treatise II, 58 blank, 59–150 An Essay on the Freedom of Wit and Humour, 151 sub-title to Treatise III, 152 blank, 153–364 Advice to an Authour, 365–6 blank.

Vol. II: 1 volume title, 2 blank, 3 sub-title to Treatise IV, 4 blank, 5–176 An Inquiry Concerning Virtue, 177 sub-title to Treatise V, 178 blank, 181–443 The Moralists, A Rhapsody, 444–6 blank.

Vol. III: π1 volume title, π1^v blank, π2 sub-title to Treatise VI, π2^v blank, 1–344 Miscellaneous Reflections, 345 sub-title to Treatise VII, 346 blank, 347–91 The Judgment of Hercules, 392 blank, 393 sub-title to Treatise VIII, 394 blank, 395–410 A Letter Concerning Design *2B2 Errata, *2B2^v blank, 2C1–2H4^v Index.

CANCELS:

Vol. I: C3 *-andum*, p. 28 l. 2 'Fair There'; *-ans*, 'Fair. There'

E1 p. 55: in the *cancellandum* the last line of p. 54 ('perfonal Merit [...] of') is repeated as the first line of p. 55; it is omitted on p. 55 of the *cancellans*.

Vol. II: I1 *-andum*, p. 122 l. 18 'on Happinefs'; *-ans*, 'no Happinefs'

Q8 *-andum*, p. 254 l. 28 'Libertine wou'd'; *-ans*, 'Libertine in Prin-'

-andum, p. 254 catchword '"ap'; *-ans*, 'ciple'

Note: Although the compositor of *cancellandum* Q8 ended with the words 'Libertine wou'd ap[prove]', so omitting the words 'in Prin[ciple]' which should have followed 'Libertine', section R begins correctly with the half word '"ciple'. This could mean that the whole of section R is a cancel.

Vol. III: D4 *-andum*, p. 43 ll. 14/15 of notes: '*nonnullis*'; *-ans*, '*nonnulli*'

-andum, p. 43 ll. 17/18 '*conjunctas*'; *-ans*, '*conjuncta*'

-andum, p. 44 l. 8 'Circumftance;', l. 17 'multiply:'; *-ans*, 'Circumftance,', 'multiply;'

(Also a number of other small changes in the notes on p. 43.)

ERRORS: Misnumeration: vol. I, '109' for 100, '343' for 243, '261' for 251, '207' for 270, '318' for 360; vol. II, main series runs 1–176 *177–8* 181–443 *444–6* (=444); '256' for 156, '290' for 280, '329' for 429; vol. III, turned '3' in 34 (sometimes), '383' for 183, '558' for 358.

Headlines: point lacking in vol. I, pp. 17, 63, 109, 155; vol. II, pp. 27, 47, 79, 93, 159, 195; vol. III, pp. 333, 335. Vol. II, pp. 42, 100, '*INQURIY*'. Vol. III, p. 37, '*EFLECTIONS*'; p. 280, '*MISCELLANEOS*'.

PLATES: Frontispiece, signed Closterman and Gribelin. Emblem on the general title, vignettes on the volume titles, and vignettes on vol. I, pp. iii, 3, 59, 153; vol. II, pp. 5, 181; vol. III, pp. 1, 345; all signed Gribelin, except the last which is signed de Matthæis and Gribelin.

PAPER: Good quality *Printing Royal* laid, no marks, size of sheet 25 × 20 in.

TYPE: Text, *English*; footnotes, *Bourgeois* leaded; Preface, *Great Primer*; index, *Bourgeois*. Vol. I, p. 41 *et passim*, Greek, probably Caslon's *Long Primer*. Vol. I, p. 59, etc., 'arabesque' ornaments.

50 LUCRETIUS, DE RERUM NATURA, 12°, 1773

TITLE-PAGE: TITI | LUCRETII CARI | DE | *RERUM NATURA* | LIBRI SEX. | [rule of 'lozenge and star' ornaments] | *BIRMINGHAMIAE :* | Typis JOHANNIS BASKERVILLE. | MDCCLXXIII.

FORMULA: Writing Medium 12° in sixes: π1 A–S⁶ ²S1 [I2, I3 and M3 unsigned]. Pp. [2] 1–131 128–214 (=218).

CONTENTS: π1 title, π1ᵛ blank, 1–214 T. Lucretii Libri Primus–Sextus (p. 100 blank).

ERRORS: Misnumeration: main series runs 1–131 128–214 (=218); '8' of 68 inverted.
Headlines: p. 17, '*LIBE R*'; pp. 87, 93 lack point.

PAPER: Medium quality *Writing Medium* laid, with 'H' and 'D' marks as in no. 45 above; size of sheet 21¾ × 17¼ in.

TYPE: Text, *Bourgeois*; pp. ²130–31, Greek, probably Caslon's *Long Primer*.

NOTE: 980 copies remained in 1775 (pp. xvii–xviii above).

51 SALLUST AND FLORUS, [HISTORIES], 4°, 1773

TITLE-PAGE: *C. CRISPUS* | SALLUSTIUS; | ET | *L. ANNAEUS* | FLORUS. | [rule of 'lozenge and star' ornaments] | *BIRMINGHAMIÆ:* | Typis JOANNIS BASKERVILLE. | MDCCLXXIII.

FORMULA: Printing Royal 4°: π1 2π1 A–2R⁴(–2R4=2π1). Pp. [4] 1–318.

CONTENTS: π1 title, π1ᵛ blank, 2π1 sub-title to Sallust, 2π1ᵛ blank (verso headlines to Sallust are C. Crispi Sallustii), 1–41 Bellum Catilinarium Cap. I–LXIV, 42 blank, 43 sub-title to Bellum Jugurth., 44 blank, 45–126 Bellum Jugurth. Cap. I–CXXII, 127 sub-title worded as π2, 128 blank, 129–77 Hist. Fragmenta Libri I–IV & Incert., 178–98 Orationes (separate verso headlines), 199 sub-title to Florus, 200 blank, 201–317 L. Annæi Flori Libri I–IV (pp. 226, 256 and 290 blank).

ERRORS: Misnumeration: '199' for 202, '102' for 203, '200' for 204, '226' for 228, '227' for 229.
Headlines: p. 12 lacks point.
Chapter numbers: p. 41, 'LXVI' for LXIV; p. 49, 'VIII' for VII; p. 251, 'XVIII' for XVII; p. 275, 'XIII' for XII.

PAPER: Three very similar lots of medium quality *Writing Royal* laid, no marks, used for A–2P, 2Q and 2R–π respectively; size of sheet 24 × 19¼ in.

TYPE: Text, *English* leaded; p. 176, *Great Primer* Greek; p. 225, etc., 'arabesque' ornaments.

NOTE: Published at a guinea; 850 copies remained in 1775 (pp. xvii–xviii above).

52 JOHN FELLOWS, HYMNS, 12°, 1773

TITLE-PAGE: HYMNS | ON | BELIEVERS BAPTISM. | [rule of 'lozenge and star' ornaments] | By *JOHN FELLOWS;* | AUTHOR of GRACE TRIUMPHANT. | [rule of 'lozenge and star' ornaments] | [plain rule] | *Then they that gladly received his word were* | *Baptized,—praifing God and having favour* | *with all the people.* Acts ii. 41. & 47. | [plain rule] | *BIRMINGHAM:* | Printed for the AUTHOR; and fold by G. KEETH, | *Grace-Church Street;* and J. DERMER, | *Shad Thames,* LONDON. | MDCCLXXIII. | [Price One Shilling.]

FORMULA: Printing Demy 12° in sixes: π^2 A–G^6 H^4. Pp. [4] 1–92.

CONTENTS: π1 title, $\pi 1^v$ blank, π2–$\pi 2^v$ Contents, 1–90 Hymns on Believers Baptism, *91–2* A Table of Scriptures, *92* advertisement for *Grace Triumphant* (12°, 'just published').

PAPER: Poor quality *Printing Demy* laid, watermark fleur-de-lys/IV, size 21¾ × 17¾ in.

TYPE: Text, *Small Pica* leaded; p. 1, 'arabesque' ornament.

NOTES: *The Monthly Review* for December 1773 (vol. XLIX, p. 505) notices what is probably this edition, although neither printer nor place of publication is named. Assigned to Baskerville on the evidence of the type.

53 CHARLES BOWLKER, THE ART OF ANGLING, SECOND EDITION, 12°, 1774

TITLE-PAGE: THE | ART of ANGLING, | AND | COMPLEAT FLY-FISHING. | Defcribing the different KINDS of FISH, their | HAUNTS, and PLACES of FEEDING and | RETIREMENT: | WITH | An ACCOUNT of the GENERATION of FISHES, | and Obfervations on the Breeding of Carps, | together with Directions how to regulate | Pools or Ponds. | ALSO | The various Kinds of BAITS adapted to each | particular Kind of FISH; and the great Di-|verfity of Flies that Nature produces in a | wonderful, yet regular Succeffion: | To which are added, | Directions for Making *Artificial Flies,* in fuch a Manner | as to have the neareft Refemblance to the *Natural:* | Illuftrated with many | *New Improvements* in the *Art* of *Angling.* | [plain rule] | THE SECOND EDITION. | [plain rule] | By *CHARLES BOWLKER,* of *Ludlow.* | [plain double rule] | *BIRMINGHAM:* | Printed by *John Bafkerville* for the Author; and fold by | *G. Robinfon,* in London; *M. Swinney,* Birmingham; | and *T. Wood,* Shrewfbury.

FORMULA: Printing Demy 12° in sixes: a^2 χ^2 B–K^6 L^4 [χ1 signed 'a3'; F3 signed 'E3', K3 sometimes signed 'L3']. Pp. i–viii 1–116.

CONTENTS: i title, ii blank, iii–iv The Preface (dated May 4, 1774), v–viii Contents, 1–116 The Art of Angling, And Compleat Fly-Fishing.

ERRORS: P. 102 numbered 'LO2'.

Headlines: lack comma on pp. 24, 38, 66 and 94; lacks point, and '*I*' for '*L*' on p. 115.

Rules of ornaments: eighth unit reversed on pp. 54, 71 and 90; eleventh unit reversed on pp. 76 and 93.

P. 87, l. 4: 'Fy' for 'Fly'.

PAPER: Poor quality *Printing Demy* laid, watermark fleur-de-lys/IV, size of sheet 21 × 17 in.

TYPE: Text, *Long Primer*; 'large rosette' and 'flower' ornaments.

NOTE: This is a revised edition of a work by Richard Bowlker (*The Art of Angling Improved*, 12°, Worcester, [? 1758]), and is actually Charles Bowlker's first edition. The 'third edition' (Swinney and Evetts, Birmingham, 1780) was a re-issue of the sheets of this 'second edition', with new title page and preface (i.e. section a), and a frontispiece.

54 JOHN FELLOWS, SIX VIEWS OF BELIEVERS BAPTISM, 12°, SECOND EDITION, 'THIRD EDITION', 1774

TITLE-PAGE: SIX | VIEWS | OF | BELIEVERS BAPTISM: | I. As an ACT of SUBLIME WORSHIP to the | ADORABLE PERSONS in the GODHEAD. | II. As a REPRESENTATION of the SUFFER-|INGS of CHRIST, his DEATH, BURIAL, | and RESURRECTION. | III. As the ANSWER or DECLARATION of | a GOOD CONSCIENCE towards GOD. | IV. As an EMBLEM of REGENERATION and | SANCTIFICATION. | V. As a POWERFUL OBLIGATION to NEW-|NESS of LIFE in a COURSE of GOSPEL OBE-|DIENCE. | VI. As a lively FIGURE of the natural | DEATH of every CHRISTIAN: | Deſigned | *As an Introduction to a* Body *of* Hymns *on* Baptiſm; | *and to be bound up with them, as a Memorial for* | *the daily uſe of all* baptized Believers *and their* | *Children, eſpecially for every Perſon that is a Candi-|date for* Believers Baptiſm: | By *JOHN FELLOWS.* | *The Second Edition.—Recommended by ſeveral Miniſters.* | *BIRMINGHAM:* | Printed for the AUTHOR; and Sold by G. KEITH, *Grace-|Church Street*; and J. DERMER, *Shad Thames,* | *London.* MDCCLXXIV. | [Price Two Pence.]

VARIANT: This title-page is also found in another state, with '*Third Edition*' for '*Second Edition*' in line 26. Nevertheless, the whole of the rest of the pamphlet, including the rest of the title-page, is from the same setting of type as the 'second edition'.

FORMULA: Printing Medium 12°: A^{12}. Pp. [2] 1–22.

CONTENTS: A1 title, A1^{v} blank, 1–21 Six Views of Believers Baptism, 22 We whose names are hereto subscribed, etc.

PAPER: Medium quality *Printing Medium* laid, watermark fleur-de-lys/IV, size of sheet 22¾ × 17¼ in.

TYPE: Text, *Long Primer* leaded; p. 1, 'large rosette' ornament.

NOTE: Ascribed to Baskerville on the evidence of the type.

55 SALLUST AND FLORUS, [HISTORIES], 12°, 1774

TITLE-PAGE: *C. CRISPUS* | SALLUSTIUS; | ET | *L. ANNÆUS* | FLORUS. | [rule of 'lozenge and star' ornaments] | *BIRMINGHAMIAE:* | Typis JOANNIS BASKERVILLE. | MDCCLXXIV.

FORMULA: Printing Demy 12° in sixes: π1 A–Z6(–Z6). Pp. [2] 1–274.

CONTENTS: π1 title, π1v blank, 1–47 C. Crispi Sallustii Bellum Catilinarium, 48 blank, 49 sub-title to Bellum Jugurth., 50 blank, 51–142 C. Crispi Sallustii Bellum Jugurth., 143 sub-title to Florus, 144 blank, 145–274 L. Annæi Flori Libri I–IV.

ERRORS: Misnumeration: '265' for 264, '275' for 274.
Sig. O is found to have its page numbers arranged in one of the following five ways:

(*a*) 117, 118, 119, 120, 121, 122, 123, 124, 125, 126, 127, 128.
(*b*) 157, 118, 119, 160, 121, 162, 163, 124, 165, 126, 127, 168.
(*c*) 157, 118, 119, 160, 161, 122, 123, 164, 165, 126, 127, 168.
(*d*) 117, 158, 159, 120, 161, 122, 123, 164, 125, 166, 167, 128.
(*e*) 117, 158, 159, 120, 121, 162, 163, 124, 125, 166, 167, 128.

The positions of the deckled edges and watermarks of the paper show that the book was printed by 'half-sheet imposition', with cutting.† What probably happened was that the forme was first set with the complete, but erroneous, series 117–28.‡ The error was not discovered until all the sheets of the edition had been printed on one side, and some of them on both sides. Then the numeration was corrected to run 157–68, and the remainder of the sheets pulled on the second side. Experiment with pencil and folded paper will show how, when a sheet so printed is cut in four and folded, any of the five series found can be produced by shuffling the outsets and insets.

Headlines: p. 148 '*ANNAI*' for '*ANNÆI*'; p. 249, 'LBIER', with broken 'I'; pp. 248, 266, broken '*Æ*' and '*L*'.

PAPER: Medium quality *Printing Demy* laid, watermark fleur-de-lys/IV, size of sheet 21¾ × 17¼ in. This paper is of poorer quality than that used for the other 12° Classics.

TYPE: Text, *Bourgeois*.

NOTE: 800 copies remained in 1775 (pp. xvii–xviii above).

56 WILLIAM HUNTER, THE ANATOMY OF THE HUMAN GRAVID UTERUS, 1°, 1774

TITLE-PAGE: ANATOMIA | UTERI HUMANI GRAVIDI | TABULIS ILLUSTRATA, | AUCTORE | GULIELMO HUNTER, | SERENISSIMAE REGINAE CHARLOTTAE MEDICO EXTRAORDINARIO, | IN ACADEMIA REGALI ANATOMIAE PROFESSORE, | ET SOCIETATUM, REGIAE ET ANTIQUARIAE, SOCIO. | BIRMINGHAMIAE EXCUDEBAT JOANNES BASKERVILLE, MDCCLXXIV. | LONDINI PROSTANT APUD S. BAKER, T. CADELL, D. WILSON, G. NICOL, ET J. MURRAY. | [rule of 'arabesque' ornaments] | *THE ANATOMY* | *OF THE* | *HUMAN GRAVID UTERUS* | *EXHIBITED IN FIGURES,* | *BY* | *WILLIAM HUNTER,* | *PHYSICIAN*

† I.e. the arrangement shown by John Johnson (*Typographia* (London, 1824), vol. II p. *17) as '*A Common Half Sheet of Twelves*'.

‡ This was not a case of failing to make the proper changes in a skeleton forme. No earlier half sheet in this book begins with p. 117; nor indeed would a sheet or half sheet of a book printed from any normal imposition (except folio) begin with this page number, unless p. 1 did *not* begin a sheet.

EXTRAORDINARY TO *THE QUEEN*, PROFESSOR OF | *ANATOMY IN THE ROYAL ACADEMY, AND FELLOW OF THE* | *ROYAL AND ANTI QUARIAN SOCIETIES.* | PRINTED AT *BIRMINGHAM* BY *JOHN BASKER VILLE*, 1774. | SOLD IN *LONDON* BY *S. BAKER* AND *G. LEIGH*, IN *York-Street; T. CADELL*, IN THE *Strand; D. WILSON* AND *G. NICOL*, | OPPOSITE *York-Buildings;* AND *J. MURRAY*, IN *Fleet-Street.*

FORMULA: Super Royal sheets, unfolded: 21 leaves + 34 plates (arranged thus: leaves 1 to 4, plate 1, leaf 5, plates 2 and 3 [back to back], leaf 6, plates 4 and 5, leaf 7—and so on up to—plates 32 and 33, leaf 21, plate 34). Unsigned, unnumbered.

CONTENTS: Leaf 1 title, 1v blank, 2 To the King, 2v blank, 3–4v Prooemium : Preface (Latin and English in parallel columns), leaves 5–21v Tabulae : Plates I–XXXIV (Latin and English in parallel columns, each page describing the plate facing it).

PLATES: Thirty-four copperplates, numbered at the foot. Signed by the artists J. van Rymsdyk, E. Edwards, A. Cozens and Blakey; and by the engravers F. S. Ravenet, G. Scotin, T. Major, R. Strange, I. S. Müller, C. Grignion, P. C. Canot, P. Maleuve, I. Mitchel, Mechel, Menil, F. Aliamet, J. Fougeron, H. Bryer, T. Worlidge and G. Powle. Plates 1, 2, 4, 6, 12, 13, 16, 20, 22, 23, 27 and 33 sometimes have the imprint '*Pub: Nov: 15: 1774, by Dr. Hunter.*' stamped or printed (in Thomas Cottrell's *Double Pica* Script type) at the bottom right, usually inside the plate mark.

PAPER: Text: medium quality *Super Royal* laid, watermark fleur-de-lys in a shield, crowned, over GR/IV, size of sheet 27 × 19 in.

Plates: each plate is on a half sheet of *Grand Eagle* laid, watermark double-headed eagle/DUPUY AUVERGNE etc. as Heawood 1317; the official size of *Grand Eagle* was 40 × 26¾ in.

TYPE: Text, *Great Primer*, *English*; Dedication, *Two-line English*, leaded.

NOTES: Published on about 5 December 1774, price six guineas in boards (*Birmingham Gazette*, no. 1725).

Lord Rothschild has a copy in which Plate 1 is printed on wove paper, and has the following imprint engraved on the plate: 'London Published July 1st 1815. by E. COX. and SON. St Thomas's Street. Borough.'; the letterpress leaves and the remainder of the plates are exactly as usual, including the 1774 imprints on Plates 2, 4, 6, etc.†

'Ballantyne's Edition' was published in 1818 at five guineas in boards; it consisted of the original letterpress leaves, without the dedication, and the plates reprinted on wove paper, plus a portrait of John Haighton, M.D.

Lithographic facsimiles of the plates were published in 1828 (not seen) and 1851, with the text reset.

† *The Rothschild Library* (Cambridge, privately printed, 1954), vol. 1, pp. 298–9 (No. 1181).

APPENDIX

A List of Books printed in Baskerville type at the Oxford University Press and by Robert Martin before 1775

Add. 1 *Η ΚΑΙΝΗ ΔΙΑΘΗΚΗ.* NOVUM TESTAMENTUM. Juxta exemplar millianum. Typis Joannis Baskerville. Oxonii: e Typographeo Clarendoniano. M DCC LXIII. Sumptibus Academiæ.

FORMULA: Writing Royal 4° in twos: π^2 A–5M^2 [π1 half-title].

NOTE: On 23 June 1761 the Delegates authorised the printing of 500 copies (Straus and Dent, p. 112).

Add. 2 *Η ΚΑΙΝΗ ΔΙΑΘΗΚΗ.* NOVUM TESTAMENTUM. Juxta exemplar millianum. Typis Joannis Baskerville. Oxonii: e Typographeo Clarendoniano. M DCC LXIII. Sumptibus Academiæ.

FORMULA: Writing Royal 8° in fours: π^2 A–4P^4 4Q^2 [π1 half-title; 2G2 signed 'Ff2'].

NOTE: On 23 June 1761 the Delegates authorised the printing of 2000 copies (Straus and Dent, p. 112).

Add. 3 THE CHASE, A POEM: To which is added Hobbinol, or the Rural Games. The Author, William Somervile, Esq;...Birmingham: Printed by Robert Martin, and Sold by A. Donaldson at his Shop, near Norfolk Street in the Strand, London. M DCC LXVII.

FORMULA: Large Printing Royal 8°: A–M^8 N^4 [A2 signed '2A'].

NOTE: First edition: 4°, London, 1735.

Add. 4 THE WORKS OF SHAKESPEAR, From Mr. Pope's Edition. Volume the First [Second] [Third] [Fourth] [Fifth] [Sixth] [Seventh] [Eighth] [Ninth]. Birmingham: Printed and sold by Robert Martin; and by R. Goadby in Sherborne, [;] M. Morgan in Lichfield, [;] T. Smith in Wolverhampton, [;] A. Donaldson in London, [;] R. Bond in Glocester, and by all Country Booksellers. MDCCLXVIII.

FORMULA: Printing Demy 12°:
Vol. I: *A*1 B–N^{12} O^{10} [L2 signed '2L', L5 signed 'L6'].
II: *A*1 B–P^{12} Q^8 [B4 signed 'A4'].
III: *A*1 χ^2 B–P^{12} Q^4 [B4 signed 'B'].
IV: A^2 B–P^{12} [K3 signed 'K5', K4 signed 'H4'; L3 unsigned].
V: B–R^{12} S^6(–S6) [F2 signed 'F3', F3 signed 'F2'].
VI: *A*1 B–S^{12} [K4, K5 unsigned].

VII: B–P^{12} Q^{6} [C2, C4, C6 signed 'G2', 'G4', 'G6'; I4 unsigned].
VIII: A–R^{12} S^{8} [B3 signed 'B2', F6 signed 'E6'; B4, B5, B6, G4, R6 unsigned].
IX: A^{4} B–T^{12} U^{6}(–U6) [G4 signed 'G5'; R5 signed on the verso; G5, G6, H6, R6, U3 unsigned].

Add. 5 THE LADY'S PRECEPTOR, or, a Letter to a Young Lady of Distinction upon Politeness. Taken from the French of the Abbé d'Ancourt, And adapted... By a Gentleman of Cambridge. ...The Sixth Edition. Birmingham: Printed by R. Martin, with Mr. Baskerville's Types, for Edward Johnson, Successor to Mr. Benjamin Dod, at No. 12 Ave-Mary-Lane, Ludgate-Street, London. M DCC LXVIII. Price 1*s.*

FORMULA: Printing Demy 8°: A^{4} B–E^{8} F^{4} [A4 advertisements].

NOTE: Martin uses four different units of a 'frond' ornament that does not appear on Baskerville's specimens nor on Martin's own specimen of *c.* 1775 (Berry and Johnson, *Catalogue*, p. 32); I have been unable to identify it.

First edition: 8°, London, 1743.

Add. 6 ELOGY ON PRINCE HENRY OF PRUSSIA. Composed by His Majesty The King of Prussia;...Birmingham: Printed for Peter Elmsly, (Successor to Mr. Vaillant) opposite Southampton-street in the Strand, London. MDCCLXVIII.
[Colophon] Printed by R. Martin, with Baskerville's types.

FORMULA: Post 8°: B–D^{8} [B1 half-title] (with frontispiece facing B2).

Add. 7 ÉLOGE DU PRINCE HENRI Par S.M. le Roi de Prusse,...à Birmingham: Et se vend à Londres, Chez Pierre Elmsly, dans le Strand. 1768.

FORMULA: Post 8°: B^{8} F^{8} [B4 signed 'F4'].

For EU product safety concerns, contact us at Calle de José Abascal, 56–1°, 28003 Madrid, Spain or eugpsr@cambridge.org.

www.ingramcontent.com/pod-product-compliance
Ingram Content Group UK Ltd.
Pitfield, Milton Keynes, MK11 3LW, UK
UKHW050106190425
457623UK00023B/360